SPIRIT IN ACTION

Teaching the Bahá'í Faith

by

Nathan Rutstein

GEORGE RONALD
OXFORD

GEORGE RONALD, Publisher
46 High Street, Kidlington, Oxford, OX5 2DN

First reprint

To the memory of Shoghi Effendi
whose indomitable spirit
galvanized the Bahá'í World

ISBN 0-85398-175-2 (Hardcover)
ISBN 0-85398-176-0 (Softcover)

Typeset by Sunrise Setting, Torquay, Devon
Printed in the United States of America

Contents

ONE

Success in Teaching

The slender young man in buffalo skin pants stained with pitch was standing under the broiling New Mexico summer sun on the shoulder of a major highway, trying to hitch a ride further west. He looked like a cowboy, but he had never rounded up a herd of cattle nor broken a wild stallion. He had made an attempt once, but had failed miserably.

Where was he going? He really didn't know. East was one direction he didn't want to go. He wanted to get away as far as possible from his home in Massachusetts. He wanted to shut out the past. His father's suicide frightened him. He had to run, to find something decent, something fresh and pure, a new way to live where gentleness, compassion and love were commonplace, where people really respected each other and found joy in serving each other. Deep down he knew there must be such a place, because he had seen in God's world patches and, at times, stretches of unimaginable beauty. It was in one of these places he wanted to dwell. He had nineteen dollars left and hadn't bathed or changed clothes in days, a far cry from his pampered upbringing in a prominent

New England home. He was determined to find what he was looking for. That determination had been evident even when he had been younger. At fourteen he called on most of the clergymen in town to see if they knew the path to the ideal place, where internal peace could be developed, where people treated each other as members of a loving family. He had found no direction from them.

The cars roared by, heading west, where perhaps his 'promised land' was. The vehicle that slowed down looked familiar to the hitchhiker. So did the driver behind the steering wheel. It was his brother. 'Why is he heading west?' he thought. 'Wasn't he leaving New Mexico for the east?'

The hitchhiker got into the car, even though he didn't want to be with anyone he knew back home, particularly the brother he was tired of competing with. The guy was older and seemed to have all the answers. Besides, he felt his brother was his parents' favorite son. That irked him. The fact that his brother was driving the car that had been bequeathed to the hitchhiker by his father bothered him also. He couldn't have it, he had been told, because he wasn't responsible enough to own an automobile.

His brother wasn't going far, only to Santa Fe to take care of some administrative matters at the college he attended, and then he was heading home, the place the hitchhiker was running away from. But he went along with his brother anyway. 'I can always get out', he thought, 'if I find a nice place on the way.'

As they drove along a highway that seemed endlessly straight, flat and black, the hitchhiker dreamt about his 'promised land', writing down his impressions, oblivious of the miles and miles of ripening wheat fields on both sides of the road.

When his brother asked what he was writing, the hitchhiker shared the outline of the kind of world he wanted to live in. A breath or two after the recitation, the hitchhiker thought aloud of starting a movement to promote the establishment of a society that would preserve human dignity in a changing world. 'What should I call it?' he asked.

'Sounds like the Bahá'í Faith', his brother replied. The brother had mentioned the Faith to him a year before, back home, at a meeting in some Bahá'í couple's home. He had refused to listen to what had been said that night because he was repelled by the idea of accepting what his brother had embraced. He was his own man, he believed, determined to benefit from his own spiritual quest.

But that had been a year ago. Now he and his brother were alone in a car. For some reason, it seemed safer to hear what his brother wanted to share with him in a car 2,000 miles from home. So the hitchhiker listened to the Bahá'í message. It matched what he had sketched out on his pad, and went far beyond what he had thought of: glorious concepts which he knew were right for the day in which he lived – and longer. It was spiritual common sense. The more he heard, the more convinced he became. He drank of the truth. Like a thirsty desert dweller, he couldn't drink enough. Time became meaningless. The real journey wasn't taking place in the car. What direction the vehicle was heading no longer mattered. His famished soul was soaring into the 'promised land' for which he had searched so long.

In Missouri, he declared his belief in Bahá'u'lláh and insisted on becoming a Bahá'í immediately. At the nearest telephone booth, his brother dialed the National Bahá'í Center in Wilmette, and the hitchhiker shared his discovery with the pleasant woman on the other end of the telephone.

The hitchhiker continued heading east with his brother, to the place he had been running away from. But he wasn't going home, because he had found his real home in Bahá'u'lláh's Revelation. Though he felt uneasy about returning to the area where he had been brought up, he no longer viewed it as a cursed place. In a way, he was returning as a triumphant explorer because he had discovered what had eluded him for as long as he could remember – the 'promised land'.

But now he had to live in it. Doing that didn't seem difficult. At least not in the beginning. Spending six weeks in the spiritually-charged atmosphere of Green Acre Bahá'í school helped. It was there that he found what makes us appreciate the 'promised land' more and more; what helps us to know ourselves better; and what gives us greater understanding of the purpose of life, as well as the inspiration to achieve it.

He immersed himself in the Creative Word, reading and rereading the *Kitáb-i-Íqán*, the *Epistle to the Son of the Wolf*, *Gleanings from the Writings of Bahá'u'lláh*, and *Prayers and Meditations*. With the few dollars he had, he purchased copies of those books, and they became his guide through the 'promised land'.

Going to college seemed to make sense. To his mother, who hadn't become a Bahá'í yet, this decision was evidence that whatever it was in which he and his brother were involved, it had the power to change people for the better. She gladly paid for her son's college tuition.

But the hitchhiker's change wasn't complete. He arrived at college in his buffalo skin pants, cowboy shirt, suspenders and boots, undoubtedly an oddity in the tranquil Vermont village where the college was located. Evidently, he wasn't aware of how others perceived him. He was wearing clothes that made him feel comfortable. Perhaps had he known what people were thinking when they saw him walking on campus, he would have dressed differently, because he wanted to fit into the mainstream of society. For so long he had stood on the edge of acceptability, even as a child, always wanting to be part of the 'gang' but never allowed to join. Maybe it was his natural free spirit that kept him on the outside. Knowing that was no consolation to someone who wanted to be like everyone else and was denied his wish. But now he had something that was lessening the pain of being denied entrance into the arena of conventionality. It was the Creative Word, a term with which he wasn't yet familiar. But to the ailing person, the name of the medicine isn't as important as what it does for him. Through daily reading and pondering of his Bahá'í books, a spiritual armor enveloped him, protecting him from insults and ridicule; and he began to take on a magnetic quality, attracting all sorts of people. In fact, in a few weeks, he became a popular person on campus, without trying to be. Many of the conventional types who aspired to be lawyers and doctors, and those who congregated on the fringe of civilization and expressed their contempt for the established order by growing very long hair, sought out the hitchhiker. He became a bridge between the two groups. Without him they avoided each other. His dormitory was dubbed 'The Persian Palace', even though no one there wore a turban or spoke the language. The only things Persian in the hitchhiker's room were the titles of some of his books, which many of his student visitors felt possessed magic. Besides, whoever heard of a Persian wearing buffalo skin pants? It was obvious even to the hitchhiker that the name given his dormitory was a term of respect and appreciation. Unlike the other campus buildings, his dormitory became known as a place where one could gain self-awareness and experience tranquility, contentment and joy. Many students gravitated to his room, at all hours of the day. The Bahá'í would read aloud passages from the *Kitáb-i-Íqán*, weaving a spell that bathed and caressed their souls. It had to be magic, they believed, because they had difficulty understanding what was being read to them. All they knew was that it sounded beautiful, so beautiful that it lifted them beyond their troubles, their self-doubts and inner pain.

Listening to the Creative Word became a pastime with some of the students, making it difficult for the Bahá'í to do his academic work. That hardship was compensated for by the steady enrollment of new believers; even a campus drug dealer flushed his cache of hashish down the toilet and signed his declaration card.

The hitchhiker's reputation spread, especially among the women. It was understandable why it did. Most young men who walked in the woods with their girl friends wouldn't recite aloud the Tablet of Aḥmad. Well, the hitchhiker did. Although startled at first, the women didn't run away. Of course, whatever romantic expectations they had were replaced by thoughts of the divine.

He had some earthly help in teaching the Faith. A Bahá'í family in town had regular firesides and study classes and learned quickly to expect the unusual from their spiritual brother on campus. One time he arrived with five newly declared students and one declaration card with five signatures.

Twenty-three students became Bahá'ís that academic year and most of them have remained firm in the Faith, living in different parts of the world, some as pioneers. As for the hitchhiker, he didn't return to the college.

The hitchhiker was never able to duplicate that teaching success, not that he didn't try. He tried hard, but it became a struggle, then a burden, and when that became too much of a strain, he gave up teaching for a while. He fluctuated between spurts of furious teaching activity and no teaching. For years he was unable to understand why that special teaching touch eluded him. At first, he rationalized, thinking that perhaps college students were more susceptible to new ideas – that conditions were different in the so-called 'real world'. But he dropped that notion after attending other colleges where he tried to teach, and had never come close to experiencing the success he had experienced in Vermont.

'Could it be', he wondered, 'that what happened at that Vermont college was a fluke?' Deep down he knew that wasn't true. Something special had been done during that year in Vermont. Certainly it had nothing to do with wearing buffalo skin pants or reciting the Tablet of Ahmad in the woods. But there were moments when he flirted with the idea of resorting to those tactics if that was what it took to regain the ability to attract lots of people to the Faith. Of course, he didn't bow to superstition, but he didn't relieve his anxiety either.

He was perplexed. After all he was a Bahá'í who went to Feasts regularly and held a fireside whenever he encountered a searching soul, and through the years he served faithfully on several Local Spiritual Assemblies. 'What went wrong?' he often asked himself.

TWO

Creating a Spiritual World

On the face of it, spiritualizing the planet and unifying humankind seem impossible. But that is what Bahá'ís are charged with doing. Certainly it is fair for objective social observers to doubt that the Bahá'ís will realize their goals. After all, every attempt in the past has failed. Human nature seems unchangeable. Even the world's superpowers, with their vast material resources, don't dare undertake what the Bahá'ís are attempting. And during their weaker moments, some believers wonder about their religion's capability to carry out such a mighty enterprise. It isn't that they don't believe in Bahá'u'lláh, but, on analysis, they deduce that the Bahá'ís are really insignificant in the world – actually puny in terms of human power and wealth. So some silently subscribe to the belief that God will have to intervene directly through some extraordinary event for the planet to be spiritualized and its inhabitants united. A reasonable assumption – but a dangerous one, because waiting for the 'apocalypse' kills enthusiasm for teaching. So much energy is committed to discerning the signs of the pending cataclysm, that there is very little left for sharing the Message of Bahá'u'lláh with others. Besides, one could rationalize, 'Why bother to teach when everything is going to cave in?' Certainly, we know that 'He doeth whatsoever He willeth, and ordaineth that which He pleaseth.'[1] But we can't predict what He will do. Nothing we try can alter that. According to Shoghi Effendi, there is that which God is doing and that which He has directed us to do through Bahá'u'lláh.[2] We can't assist God in carrying out the plan He has chosen to unfold alone. What we are supposed to be doing is to fulfill the divine plan which is part of Bahá'u'lláh's Revelation. By following it, much will be achieved in spiritualizing and unifying the human family.

The Organic Nature of the Faith

Success, however, hinges on the believers' understanding that their Faith is organic in nature. It grows. It doesn't expand. Much like the difference between planting an oak tree and building a brick wall. From the tree, another one springs up, and from it still another, until – in time – a forest exists.

In a sense a Bahá'í is like a seed, possessing powerful potential for spiritual growth. With proper cultivation, growth occurs; radiance replaces despair, and the Bahá'í attracts the Holy Spirit – and seekers. As he grows, he becomes more attractive and more dependent on Bahá'u'lláh's Revelation in negotiating every aspect of his life. He is involved in a cycle whereby devotion to regular prayer and study of the Writings draws him further into the world of the spirit where a sense of security and well-being reinforces his growing desire to pray and deepen. This continues until he begins to recognize and appreciate the power of the Revelation.

Because of this power the only Bahá'í on a tiny island in the Pacific Ocean is potentially a group, a Local Spiritual Assembly and a community. In other words, the growth of the Faith on that island, or any other place, is partly dependent on the spiritual growth of the believer there. If he grows, others should eventually notice. He will be keenly aware of the need to teach – and want to do it. A group will be formed. Imagine all the new Bahá'ís integrating prayer and deepening into their lives. In time, an Assembly will be established. As the new Bahá'ís pray, deepen and teach, even more seekers will embrace the Faith, creating a community. Eventually some Bahá'ís will be inspired to go elsewhere to teach the Faith. One might go to a neighboring village; another might go to live on the other side of the island; someone might venture to a different land. All would go with the intent of being the cause of raising new Assemblies.

It seems so simple – doesn't it? Well, it is. The trouble lies with execution, generating desire and energy to put into practice the clearly enunciated Teachings of our Faith. A deeply entrenched pattern of behavior developed prior to becoming a Bahá'í, attachments to, elements of an unspiritual society that is sinking, and years of cultural immersion are a few obstacles that make execution difficult. Bahá'ís everywhere, especially in the Western world, are confronted, even plagued, by them. Overcoming them is a struggle, as most Bahá'ís can attest. But they are not insurmountable. In fact, where Bahá'ís triumph over inertia and develop confidence in the Teachings and in themselves, individual and collective growth will occur. But the desire and confidence cannot be sustained if the Bahá'í stops perfecting himself. He is seized by apathy.

The Growth of the Faith

Despite the spiritual battles that Bahá'ís face every day, their Faith grows steadily around the world. Much progress has been made since 1844, especially when you consider how widespread it is today. If you were to spin one of those metal globes usually found in geography classrooms, and place a finger on some land mass, little or big, chances are Bahá'ís are there. Even those who never had an interest in geography before embracing the Faith have developed one, because when we learn of Bahá'ís living in remote places like Vanuatu and Banjul, in Spitsbergen, in Punta Arenas, or Moose Jaw, Saskatchewan, we want to know where they are located. When we discover there are now people who believe what we believe living on a couple of dots in the Indian Ocean, on a bit of land above the Arctic Circle, in the world's southernmost municipality, in the wilds of Canada, we are impressed, and those lingering doubts about the Faith's ability to carry out its mission vanish. Our imagination is stirred. Our mind's eye opens; and for a few rare moments we sense the glorious long-range future. It becomes apparent that we are participating in the development of the foundation of a world civilization envisioned by Bahá'u'lláh; and we begin to understand how from it will evolve 'The Most Great Peace', a condition longed for by the ancients and by men and women of today.

We realize that to invest energy in hoping for some cosmic event that would, in a flash, spiritually enlighten everyone and unite humanity, is a waste of precious time that could be spent on pursuing the process that Bahá'u'lláh assures us will lead to the building of the Kingdom of God on earth, namely the spiritualizing of oneself and sharing the Message with others. The Cause of God is a grassroots movement; it leaps from heart to heart. That is, essentially, how the Faith has spread to more than 112,000 localities. It grows through individual effort, mostly by ordinary people, not through some super-charismatic evangelist or corps of them. In the Bahá'í Faith everyone is a teacher. With the passing of each Central Figure, growth has accelerated instead of diminishing. At the time of the Báb's martyrdom, the Cause of God was established in two nations; with the passing of Bahá'u'lláh, it was established in fifteen countries; in 1921, when the Master passed away, the Faith had taken root in thirty-five nations. Through Shoghi Effendi's guidance, it had been established in more than 250 countries and territories. By 1982 it was established in more than 350 countries and territories – including dependencies – and represented in more than 2,000 ethnic groups. Imagine how wide-spread, how well established the Faith will be in 1992, in 2022, in 2062, and a century later. It grows like the movement of a mighty river, starting as a stream in an obscure woodlands and becoming broader and deeper as it flows towards the ocean.

Hard work on the part of thousands of Bahá'ís over a 140-year period is the basis for the Faith's remarkable growth. For most of us the hardest work is disciplining ourselves to function in every way and at all times as a Bahá'í. For some, this has led to torture, imprisonment and death by firing-squad. But hard work is rewarded, as it is in professional, artistic and athletic endeavors; except that the Bahá'í's reward does not come in the form of wage increases or bronze plaques, trophies or medals. To a Bahá'í the greatest reward is to witness a fellow human being discover Bahá'u'lláh and embrace Him. Watching joy encompass a new believer is thrilling, but knowing there is another enthusiastic worker for Bahá'u'lláh is a reward of special significance. Could there be any greater reward to a Bahá'í than to have participated in teaching a soul the Faith? Not really – because there is another human being on the planet with a world consciousness, with an awareness of the importance of overcoming one's prejudices, with access to a special source for spiritual growth, and who is willing to work to develop a divinely conceived world order. What the new believer represents is progress in pulling together the human family and establishing real world peace, something Bahá'ís want more than anything else.

How the Faith Grows: Plans and Goals

Although the Faith generally grows on a one-to-one basis, there are exceptions. When the 4,000 inhabitants of an island off the coast of India became Bahá'ís at the same time, the believer who took the message there probably never thought that he could be the cause of such a stupendous victory. Undoubtedly he was drawing upon the power of the Revelation – probably his only resource. As incredible as that teaching feat was, 'Abdu'l-Bahá points out that a single soul is capable of guiding a nation.[3]

Regardless of whether a believer attracts one soul or thousands, what is most important is the process used in achieving teaching success. Forces greater than ourselves

will determine the number of people who become
Bahá'ís. Worrying over how many men and women to
enroll usually generates anxiety and the quality of our
praying and deepening deteriorates. By concentrating on
our basic spiritual responsibilities, the right results will
come. We will be helped in a number of ways. Our
sincere prayers will be answered and we will receive
concrete divine direction in the form of plans. With a plan
to work with, we will be able to focus on goals, thus
avoiding the anxiety and frustration that results from the
hit-and-miss approach to teaching and community
development. Knowing that the plans we received from
the Guardian, and currently receive from the Universal
House of Justice, are divinely conceived is a comfort and
an inspiration, because we know that we cannot fail if we
sincerely follow them, and that by achieving their goals
humanity is drawn closer to the 'Most Great Peace'.

Actually, these plans are phases of a grand plan. With
the fulfillment of each phase, another one is unveiled,
usually consisting of more challenging goals than before.
One thing is certain: when the present phase is
completed, another will follow it. This process will go
on for a long time, perhaps hundreds of years or more,
until the grand plan is fulfilled and God's Kingdom on
Earth is established.

Every plan conceived at the World Center takes into
account each national community's spiritual maturity as
well as the economic, social and political condition of the
land, and the government's attitude towards the Faith.
Because the situation of each Bahá'í national community
is different, the nature and number of goals differ for
every National Spiritual Assembly. Obviously, where
the Faith is suppressed, not as much is asked of that

country's Assembly as of one where the Faith is free to grow. Also, a newly-formed Assembly, or a struggling one, doesn't receive the kind of goals a well-established Assembly does. In other words, the Universal House of Justice gives each National Assembly what it believes each one has the capacity to achieve.

The allocation of goals begins with the International Teaching Centre in Haifa, which is composed of all the Hands of the Cause of God and the Counsellors (at present, nine) assigned to the Holy Land. From studying every report of the Continental Boards of Counsellors, the Centre gains an understanding of the spiritual and administrative condition of each national community. The Counsellors, based in different zones in the world, gain their understanding of the Bahá'í situation in their areas of responsibility from periodic reports from their Auxiliary Board members for protection and propagation, who, in turn, are briefed by their Assistants on a regular basis. While gathering data on the Bahá'í condition in each country, the International Teaching Centre is busy trying to determine what the non-Bahá'í condition is like in each country. After evaluating both sets of information, it puts together a suggested list of goals for each National Spiritual Assembly, which it submits to the Universal House of Justice. From the material supplied by the Centre, from its own information related to each community which it receives from reports and recommendations of the National Assemblies, and after consultation with the International Teaching Centre, the Universal House of Justice adopts a plan for the Bahá'í world community.

Obviously, the Guardian didn't have the kind of support that exists in the World Centre today. In devising a plan, he relied heavily on National Assembly minutes. When he unveiled the first Seven Year Plan to the United States in 1937, there were no living Hands of the Cause, no Counsellors, no Auxiliary Board members or Assistants. There were only eight National Spiritual Assemblies and a few Local Spiritual Assemblies, the majority of them plagued with the kind of problems most fledgling institutions suffer from. He didn't allow the immaturity of the Assemblies to deter him from setting in motion the mechanism for further collective growth in the Faith. He knew that in time – through prayer and deepening – the infant institutions, often wobbly and fumbling, would grow stronger and one day evolve into Houses of Justice. Certainly the goals of the first Seven Year Plan pale in comparison with the International Seven Year Plan launched in 1979. In forty-two years considerable growth had taken place: 135 National Spiritual Assemblies and more than 25,000 Local Spiritual Assemblies. It's not hard to conceive that the number will be a lot higher in 2014!

As meager as the goals of the plan launched in 1937 seem today, the Guardian viewed them as the farmer views seeds during planting season. The first Seven Year Plan would eventually yield its expected harvest.

Having one believer in the sparsely populated state of Vermont was one goal of the first Seven Year Plan. That goal was achieved. And the long-range effect of that victory is now seen. In 1982 Vermont had six Local Spiritual Assemblies and twenty-one groups. Not as dramatic a growth as in South Carolina, Florida, Oregon and California; but the Cause of God is growing in an area of the United States where a change of belief is a slow, methodical, often painful process.

Every time a goal is won history is made, because a beleaguered and unaware humanity is drawn closer to the formation of a world civilization. Granted, this progress is not discernible to the naked eye, but it is progress nevertheless. At this point in the development of the Faith, historians cannot appreciate what is happening in Vermont and in thousands of other places in the world. But there will come a time when historians will take notice, and in tracing the origin and process of the unfoldment of the Cause of God they will be overcome with astonishment. Then they will appreciate the significance of a Five Year Plan (1973 to 1978) goal of having at least one believer in each county in the American state of Pennsylvania.

Opening some of the counties was extremely difficult. In fact, some of the Bahá'ís felt that it would take a miracle for someone to embrace the Faith in a place like Perry County, sparsely populated with mostly farm families steeped in Christianity and naturally resistant to social, and especially religious, change. The Pennsylvania District Teaching Committee asked one of its area representatives, who lived closer to Perry County than any other Bahá'í in the state, to take on what appeared to be an impossible task – to bring in that one, much-needed believer.

The representative, a middle-aged woman who worked odd hours, accepted the responsibility even though she wondered whether she was capable of carrying it out successfully. She was aware of the obstacles, especially her shortcomings. She wasn't a learned person, an eloquent speaker, a scholar of Christian subjects. And she lived about thirty miles from the Perry County line, which meant considerable traveling.

She prayed and meditated on her assignment. Then she thought of her friend's farm, which was in the county. In fact, there was a hill on the property overlooking the town of Newport. She could go there on a regular basis and pray that some heart would open to Bahá'u'lláh. For nearly six months, even in the snow, she drove to that hill and prayed. Then one day she received a phone call from the District Teaching Committee stating that they had just received a letter from the National Center about a young lady from Newport, Pennsylvania who had written for Bahá'í literature, having heard of the Faith through the Seals and Crofts musical group.

The area representative contacted the inquirer, who was excited about meeting a Bahá'í. In a few weeks she embraced the Faith and Perry County had another potential group, Assembly and community.

THREE

Overcoming Fear

In the Faith we hear so much about teaching that sometimes, in our weaker moments, we view it as an intrusion, and wonder if perhaps it would be better to have a special corps of trained Bahá'í teachers who would spend most of their time teaching and do nothing else professionally. With a regular cadre, it would be easier to gauge results; and so much valuable time and energy wouldn't have to be directed to stimulate believers to teach. Teaching programs would be operated efficiently; and the rank-and-file Bahá'í could pursue his career, serve on committees, maybe on a Local Spiritual Assembly, contribute to the Fund, attend Feasts regularly, and not have to feel guilty about not teaching.

Such thinking is understandable in light of the demands that are made on us today, and the pressures generated by a world that seems headed towards annihilation. The atmosphere is charged with uncertainty and fear; and this is reflected in people's faces, even those who live in rural areas. There seems to be no escape.

Through teaching, however, we are able to protect ourselves from being overwhelmed by those pressures;

we receive divine help. 'The unseen divine assistance', said the Master, 'encompasseth those who deliver the message.'[4] Teaching is essential for our spiritual growth. Ignore it and we aren't assisted, no matter how busy we are as Bahá'ís.

Today's appeal to teach is really a divine echo, raised in 1844. The Báb, Bahá'u'lláh, 'Abdu'l-Bahá, Shoghi Effendi and now the Universal House of Justice have all urged us to teach. The appeal is not a commandment, but is made as a physician prescribing a remedy to a patient. Bahá'u'lláh is a Divine Physician, whose prescription is perfect, and teaching is part of it. By teaching, we not only grow healthier, but we serve in the most meaningful way, applying the Divine Remedy to others who aren't aware of it and who are groping for help.

In Bahá'u'lláh's Dispensation the clergy is considered an outdated institution. Humanity has grown up. People are encouraged to seek truth independently. Preaching is forbidden. A clergy would impede the movement toward planetary unity. Intellectual feuding and jealousy and the drive for power would cause factionalism. Interpretation of the Creative Word would lead to the development of conflicting theologies and dogmas.

With Bahá'u'lláh's coming all things were made new; a heavenly breath of spirituality was unleashed into the world. The responsibility for teaching the Word of God was seized from the ecclesiastics and given to all, the unschooled as well as the learned. This is an appealing principle, which has liberated many from religious orthodoxy, superstition and ignorance. Through deepening and prayer we are armed with a power that can move even the most erudite into Bahá'u'lláh's embrace.

It was a rural Iranian blacksmith who could barely read

and write who taught the Faith to Mírzá Abu'l-Faḍl, one of the greatest Muslim thinkers around the turn of the century who later became the most outstanding Bahá'í scholar of his day.[5]

Fear of Teaching

It isn't easy for people brought up in a culture where only the clergy teach religion. Signing a Bahá'í enrollment card isn't going to strip away years of conditioning. We soon find ourselves grappling with doubts about our ability to teach, thinking about all the schooling priests, ministers and rabbis receive to qualify as religious teachers; and then we focus on our own inadequacies and we shrink at the thought of teaching. And sometimes our love for Bahá'u'lláh compounds the problem, because we are afraid of misrepresenting the Faith.

Hebe Struven, the younger sister of the illustrious Lua Getsinger, had doubts about her ability to teach the Faith she loved deeply. She was especially timid about giving talks, and the thought of giving one in a formal religious setting like a church petrified her. The few times she had given a formal presentation on the Faith, she had either memorized a prepared script or read from it.

When Hebe learned that Lua was going on pilgrimage to meet the Master, she begged to go along.

Aboard the ship headed for the Holy Land, Hebe prayed that she would not fall apart emotionally when introduced to 'Abdu'l-Bahá. She thought about the wonder and bounty of basking in His light: meeting Him would be the acme of personal attainment.

How radiant Lua was in the presence of the Master. Hebe stood close to her sister, practically touching her, and was startled when 'Abdu'l-Bahá turned to her and said that when speaking about the Cause of God she should let go, be free, speak from the heart and think of Him, for He would be with her to help.

'Abdu'l-Bahá had penetrated her soul, had addressed a secret fear. Before meeting Him, she had sensed that He had that power, but to be a recipient of it was an experience she would never forget. He was truly the Master.

A few days after her return from pilgrimage, the minister of the largest church in her home town called on her, asking if she would give a talk to his congregation about her experiences in the Holy Land. Her first impulse was to decline the invitation, but her spirit prevailed and she accepted it.

Hebe was terrified and at times scolded herself for saying she would speak. Of course, she remembered what the Master had told her, but in a weakened state she pleaded for forgiveness and decided to cheat a little bit. Hebe wrote an introduction to her talk, which she memorized. By doing that, she felt, she would be launched into her talk – it was something that would bolster whatever confidence she had.

The church was packed. She was on the platform with the minister, peering at the crowd and growing more nervous. Noticing the elders of the church seated in the front row, unsmiling and dressed in black suits, didn't help her state of mind. After the preacher's introduction, Hebe stood on wobbly legs, facing the audience. Her fright heightened when she couldn't remember what she had memorized. She felt naked and dumb. She noticed the clock high above the last pew; her pilgrimage came to mind; then 'Abdu'l-Bahá's face, and she thought of what He had told her, and she spoke, sharing with the audience the first thing that came to her, the title of a popular song: 'It is Springtime in the Rockies'. She paused and went on to add with greater confidence, 'And it is springtime in the world.' The rest was about the Faith and 'Abdu'l-Bahá. From that day on she always spoke from the heart when asked to speak about the Cause, always remembering 'Abdu'l-Bahá and His promise.

Lack of confidence usually generates timidity, and we hesitate to teach. It's not easy to build up our confidence when for years we have been aware of our inadequacies; especially when others, even those close to us, have pointed them out in subtle and, at times, overt ways. What is easier is to develop confidence in Bahá'u'lláh. This was emphasized in a letter written on behalf of Shoghi Effendi: 'At all times we must look at the greatness of the Cause, and remember that Bahá'u'lláh will assist all who arise in His service. When we look at ourselves, we are sure to feel discouraged by our short-comings and insignificance.'[6]

Relying on Bahá'u'lláh

If we have confidence in Bahá'u'lláh, then we will call upon Him for help, certain it will come. A student at Mills College in Oakland, California, discovered just that one day while she was in the campus chapel alone, sorrow-filled, wishing her life would end. She ran to the altar, draping herself over it. In tears, she pleaded with Bahá'u'lláh to make her a teacher of His Cause. A few seconds after that prayer lifted from her heart, the chapel doors opened, and a young man entered, obviously surprised. She walked towards him, radiant. Soon they were in a discussion, and she mentioned the Faith. He asked probing questions; and she answered with expressions she would never have thought of. What flowed from her amazed her – it was so profound.

The more we rely upon Bahá'u'lláh, the more sensitive we become about when it is the right time to mention the Faith. The same Mills College student developed that ability. It manifested itself one day while walking with two Bahá'í friends on campus. She noticed two young men sitting on the grass. She was attracted to them, feeling that she had to share the Faith with them. Had she not been with her friends she would have made the approach without any hesitation. She was afraid that her friends would think her crazy if she did what she wanted to do. But the pull towards those men was overwhelming; so she stopped, telling the Bahá'ís that she would meet them at the tea shop in ten minutes.

At first both men appeared uneasy as she approached. When she mentioned the Faith to them, one of them grew hostile; the other one's eyes began to glow, as if he had discovered a treasure. His companion soon left, and he escorted the young woman to the tea shop where they continued their discussion with the two other Bahá'ís.

The young man attended every fireside he knew of. In two years, he was pioneering in Madagascar where he now serves as an Auxiliary Board member.

The Need for Detachment

We enjoy hearing stories about teaching success because we want our Cause to succeed, and it inspires those of us who seem trapped in a community where no teaching progress is being made. 'At least some community is making headway', we think.

Although we yearn to hear more stories, we usually doubt that we could experience anything like them. 'It couldn't happen to me', we say to ourselves, because a fear that we don't want to address yet is within us. This fear prevents us from bursting forth, free and selfless, our hearts overflowing with the love of God, and wanting more than anything else to share the Message of Bahá'u'lláh.

It is the fear of being rejected that paralyzes us. Having someone we respect, even admire, respond negatively to the Faith might embarrass us, maybe humiliate us, for there is always the chance of being considered a fool for believing in something so unconventional, so strange-sounding. In the final analysis, rejection of something as precious as our Faith – a force that makes us what we are – is felt as rejection of ourselves. The pain is sharper when someone we like rejects the Message, and we doubt whether we could endure a similar encounter. So we avoid teaching in familiar places, which is usually the town where we live.

Overcoming the fear of rejection takes detachment, a condition mentioned frequently at Bahá'í study classes and often pondered when alone. For most of us, it appears to be a state beyond our grasp. But it is not. It is a condition every Bahá'í can attain. Becoming detached is a relative process. It doesn't usually come instantly. It develops over a period of time through a commitment to prayer and deepening. The more detached we are, the less pain or embarrassment we will feel when our teaching effort is rejected. The more detached we become, the less events of a collapsing world order will bother us and the more strength and courage we will have to help build a new world order where the kinds of social suffering we witness today will no longer exist. Through detachment, 'Abdu'l-Bahá points out how strong our faith can grow and how effective we can become as teachers:

'If one is turned toward heavenly things he will become like a rock. But if his heart be attached to anything in this world it will become subject to change. Attachments are like ropes which drag us to the earth when we try to fly. To be detached is to be free, is to be flying in a new ether, is to be light, is to be joyous – and a Bahá'í should be joyous. He should attain to such a station of joy that the world will inquire as to his secret. If he be entirely detached and emptied of self he will be enabled to start in a cold heart a great fire.'[7]

Throughout his life of devoted Bahá'í service, Louis Gregory exhibited detachment, enabling him to do things that others considered courageous and heroic. Some weak souls felt that Mr Gregory was insane for teaching in America's southland in the late 1920s and 30s where blacks who deviated from established social customs were lynched. They expected one day to read about him having been found dead, hanged from a tree. But he heeded his heart. Not only did he go to the deep South to teach the Faith, but he sought out a white man to accompany him. Black and white together, he felt, would exemplify what he was trying to share in his talks. In the eyes of his friends and critics, Louis Gregory was able to achieve what was considered impossible. He was able to help people in a racially segregated society to embrace Bahá'u'lláh, and by doing so to accept the principle of racial unity and harmony. What he did wasn't easy. There were threatening incidents, but he pushed on with what he believed was the right thing to do. His primary focus was on the Creative Word and the Divine standards. From them he gained assistance, and what appeared as dangerous to others, he viewed as simply surmountable hurdles. He felt protected and was a living example of what the Master once wrote: 'If one arises to promote the Word of God with a pure heart, overflowing with the love of God and severed from the world, the Lord of Hosts will assist him with such a power as will penetrate the core of existent beings.'[8]

Through prayer and deepening we generate the desire and enthusiasm to teach. We are ready to go forth. But doing it takes a surge of courage, something we will get if we specifically pray for it. The first venture may be awkward, but the more we share the Message, the less fearful we become, until teaching becomes a comfortable, enjoyable experience, something we just have to do to keep happy.

Reasons Why We Do Not Teach

Some of us pray and attempt to deepen regularly and yet resist teaching, causing an inner conflict. We find ourselves bursting with spiritual energy, but reluctant to share what we believe, because deep down we feel that teaching smacks of proselytizing. Yet we are aware of the divine exhortations to teach; and we feel guilty about not venturing forth with the Word. But we also remember how repugnant it can be to be pounced upon by a religious zealot who tries to convert us. Many of us left our churches and synagogues because we resented a clergyman telling us what we should and should not do. We accepted Bahá'u'lláh because the Bahá'ís never pressured us, and we were encouraged to investigate the truth for ourselves.

By teaching we fear we may violate an individual's

right to seek truth in his own way and within his own time frame. We may be accused of coercing people and doing the very thing we abhorred in fanatics who tried to convert us.

On the other hand, we know what Bahá'u'lláh truly represents to humanity, and we want everyone to partake of His wholesome medicine. We know how the world condition would change if that were to happen. Just thinking about that possibility excites us. Yet we hesitate to teach, hoping instead for some kind of universal mechanism or supernatural event to open people's eyes and hearts and sweep them into the Faith. This may be one of the reasons why so many of us prefer involvement with proclamation campaigns rather than teaching. It is safer to develop media materials or organize public meetings than to tell someone about the Faith and possibly offend him.

Another fear exists in some communities. It isn't discussed, because it is counter to the spirit and the letter of the Faith. In fact, it is such a flagrant violation of Bahá'í principles that no one would dare admit that he harbors such a fear. Nevertheless it exists, strangling some communities. But the strangulation is not apparent to the believers there, because everyone seemingly gets along well. In fact, they get along so well that deep down they don't want any newcomers, feeling that what has been established would be upset. They rationalize the lack of numerical growth by stressing community unity above all else. But what supposedly constitutes unity is really uniformity. There is a noticeable absence of diversity. If there is teaching, it is done half-heartedly, enough to satisfy an urgent appeal made by the National Spiritual Assembly from time to time. Undoubtedly those who harbor such a fear love Bahá'u'lláh, and some are sincere in their concern to shield their religion from being infiltrated by unwholesome elements with suspected serious social problems that might damage their religion's reputation. Often this fear stems from prejudices developed before becoming a Bahá'í. Although we are aware of the Faith's position on prejudice, and will easily share it with an inquirer and give talks on the subject, somehow we don't feel it applies to us. Yet it does. Shoghi Effendi made that clear in *The Advent of Divine Justice*. It is rare to find anyone who is free of prejudice. Through the Revelation of Bahá'u'lláh, however, we can chip away successfully at it.

Overcoming Prejudice

The healthiest Bahá'í community is one that is striving to be composed of people of different religious backgrounds, different ages, economic and social levels, and different ethnic backgrounds – all struggling to put the Teachings into practice. Obviously, with such a diverse mix of people, cultural clashes may create messy problems. But if the Faith is used to solve the problems, we will demonstrate – often through much growing-pain – to ourselves and to a skeptical world that human nature can change, that unity in diversity can be achieved, that there is a chance, a good chance, that the human family can be united; and skeptics will become seekers, even believers.

If functioning properly, each Bahá'í community is, in microcosm, a world united, and every time a community reaches such a condition, humanity draws a little bit closer to planetary unity.

Ideally, a Bahá'í welcomes diversity with open arms, knowing that in the long run the community will benefit from it. Those sincerely involved in the struggle to learn to respect different customs and different ways of thinking will eventually shed their prejudices; and people who once distrusted and disliked each other will celebrate each other's differences instead of silently cursing them. Isn't this the path that Bahá'u'lláh urges us to follow?

As Bahá'ís we know we have a mandate to grow spiritually and through that life-long effort become the means of uniting people who are suspicious of each other because they appear different and do things differently. Imagine what power will be generated in a community made up of Bahá'ís of all strata of society who are genuinely drawing strength from the Revelation to strip away their prejudices. But recognizing that such a condition can exist won't make it occur in an instant. Achieving a prejudice-free condition isn't easy. It took many years to fashion our attitudes, and it may take an equal amount of time to remove every vestige of prejudice from us. What is important is to make a genuine effort to rid ourselves of prejudice. For a Bahá'í, it should become a personal commitment. Then help comes, sometimes in strange ways, as a wealthy woman, with many years of meritorious service for the Faith, discovered in India, thousands of miles from home.

She was a perfectionist, a super-achiever who had little tolerance for ignorance, sloth and shoddy work. The people she respected most were like herself; and she had difficulty accepting others. To her credit, she was aware of this flaw. The fact that Bahá'u'lláh demands that we overcome our prejudices fired her determination to become accepting of all people. But knowing what is right is no guarantee that one does what is right.

Officially, she and her husband were in India as guests of the government's Central Handicrafts Board, helping to establish small businesses based on the country's natural resources.

Somehow the Bahá'í homefront pioneer in Bangalore discovered that the American couple were in India. So he asked his National Spiritual Assembly to urge the Americans to come to his city to deepen the friends and to help with his community's teaching effort. The man had left his native Bombay because of the Master's appeal to the large number of believers of Zoroastrian background in that city to settle elsewhere in India.

It was a hot, muggy day when they stepped off the airplane in Bangalore. A government limousine was waiting for them at the airport. After checking into their air-conditioned room at the posh government house (a place where visiting dignitaries stay), they asked their chauffeur to drive them to an address that had been scribbled on a piece of paper.

When they reached the street, the chauffeur proceeded by foot to find the place where the pioneer to Bangalore lived. In a few minutes the man was found standing in the muddy road in front of his humble restaurant, waving to the Americans as they approached. As the couple got closer they noticed that the man's seersucker suit was rumpled, that his eyes were crossed and that his hair stood on end like a porcupine. He was no more than five feet tall and chubby.

Evidently, the American man sensed what his wife was thinking for he said to her, 'If that's what the Bahá'ís in this city are like then we must accept it.'

As the Bahá'í pioneer to Bangalore embraced her

husband, the woman was nearly overcome by the powerful odor of onion radiating from the man. That gentleman was elated to see his fellow believers from America. He had hoped they would come to his city but wasn't sure that such important people would take the time to do that. The Americans' coming was attributed to the Will of God.

After the greetings, the smiling man asked the couple to come back in about seven hours to meet some of the friends in his home, which was behind the restaurant. He had to hurry because assembling the believers wasn't easy. Not many could afford a telephone.

After resting and refreshing themselves in their air-conditioned room, the Americans returned to the pioneer's home. When they went through the door between the restaurant and the man's living quarters, they were astonished. Seventy or eighty people were crammed into the room, all sitting respectfully in chairs. It was the kind of mixture of human beings that would have brought joy to 'Abdu'l-Bahá. Some of them resembled those who had stood in front of their shacks earlier in the day gawking at the couple. Others were highly educated. In fact, there were a few who had been connected with the official court of the Maharaja of Mysore, the province where Bangalore is located. One of them had been the Maharaja's treasurer. Everyone in the room was a Bahá'í, attracted to the Faith by the squat, cross-eyed man who had placed himself in an obscure corner of the room.

It was obvious that everyone in that place loved the Bahá'í pioneer to Bangalore, that they sensed something in him that the Americans were beginning to appreciate. They had come to Bangalore to deepen the friends, but it was difficult to speak, because they were choked with emotion. In the dim light of the room, they could barely see the Bahá'í pioneer to Bangalore, but with their inner eyes they recognized what the others there already knew.

FOUR

Awakening the Desire to Teach

Trying to force ourselves to teach can be counter-productive. It may result in a short-lived furious spurt, followed by a long stretch of trying to recover from the effort, but not succeeding because of guilt. And it seems that the longer we stay away from teaching the more guilty we become until, out of self-defense, we plunge into an escape activity, avoiding any mention of or involvement in teaching. Spiritual inertia sets in and we become estranged from the Faith, even though we continue to believe in Bahá'u'lláh. A deep conflict flares up. It is so deep that it is out of reach. But we know it exists, because of a continual, indescribable ache in the heart that grows more pronounced when we are left alone with our thoughts.

We know the ache could disappear if we started teaching. But we resist taking the step, because we secretly resent being reminded about the need to teach. The stream of correspondence urging the intensification of teaching may be read out of duty; but what is communicated to us is construed as nagging. The word 'teach' becomes offensive. At times we interpret the appeal to teach as a shrill screech of desperation. And we view that as undignified, something the Cause of God should never stoop to.

This painful state of mind, usually not shared with anyone else, results from a lack of understanding of what teaching is and why Bahá'ís must teach. Doing something blindly, even if the request or appeal is issued by someone prominent or by an important institution, can easily spawn doubts, especially in a person who tends to think independently. If we had the choice, most of us would prefer knowing the reason why we should carry out an obligation, even one that is divine.

There are institutionally-organized remedies for awakening interest in teaching, but they rarely have a long-lasting effect. From highly-spirited conferences an emotionally-charged atmosphere is generated, infusing in us an enthusiasm for teaching. Two weeks later, back in the world of earning a living and paying bills, our enthusiasm wanes and teaching is relegated to a low position on our personal 'things-to-do' priority list.

We wonder if perhaps more teaching conferences could prevent that from happening. But organizing successful conferences takes time, money and lots of mental and physical energy. Besides, the friends would tire from too many meetings and attendance would dwindle. And there is always the danger of the believers feeling like tired horses being flogged.

Ideally, the desire to teach should come from within us, not from outside stimulation. For that to happen a true understanding of what teaching is and why we must teach is needed. Without that understanding we usually run out of stamina and interest, and instead of behaving as a Bahá'í teacher should, we behave like a religious salesman or a zealot, an approach that can hurt a seeker, give the wrong impression of our Faith and damage its reputation. Many of us have participated in teaching efforts where we questioned our motives and approaches, but went ahead anyway, because we felt it was more important to help the community overcome a crisis which had become apparent about a month before Riḍván. Our teaching goals hadn't been achieved. Guilt, and pleas from district or provincial teaching committees stirred us into action, obsessed with accomplishing our tasks and giving little attention to the way we carried them out. Often the results of our efforts were proof that what we had done wasn't right, but we kept our feelings to ourselves. We had new believers who didn't know who Bahá'u'lláh was, and some who had signed a declaration card thinking they were joining a progressive social club or subscribing to a magazine.

Deep down we knew that what we had done was not what Bahá'u'lláh meant by teaching, and vowed never to do it again, but usually we relented when another plea was made. And every time we engaged in such a frenetic campaign, the conflict raging within us was reinforced, creating an unhealthy attitude towards teaching.

The Relationship between Prayer and Teaching

Teaching is much more than the act of telling someone about the Faith or holding a fireside. Those are only aspects of the process. Teaching is an expression of the Bahá'í meaning of faith. It is a growing awareness and understanding of the Teachings, translated into action in every phase of life. In other words, teaching is a state of mind. By 'state of mind' is meant a perpetual desire to attract people to the Cause, not always apparent to the beholder because the Bahá'í has career and family responsibilities that must be considered. Nevertheless, it is a part of him, operating like a dynamic emotional current that accelerates when an obvious opportunity presents itself to share the Message; at that point he's aware of the internal yearning. Other times the current remains operating on a subconscious level, unnoticed by the beholder, but usually sensed by the true seeker, for there's an attractive gleam in the Bahá'í's eyes, an appealing glow to his face. In other words, the teaching state of mind is 'living the life', a condition that comes about from an active commitment to regular prayer and deepening. As the state of mind develops, an impulse for action results as naturally as a young plant emerges from the seed, breaks through the ground and stretches toward the sun.

This process became apparent to an American college teacher in a mysterious way. It was mysterious only because he couldn't foresee what would unfold and when, nor could he fathom the dynamics that had led to the extraordinary change of heart within him.

After learning about the importance to teaching of prayer and deepening, he decided to try it every day, as Bahá'u'lláh prescribes. Close to six months had elapsed when, after class one day, he had an urge to have lunch at the student-run restaurant on campus, a place he had avoided because of its noisy, smoky atmosphere and junky food. He had been a devoted nutrition-conscious eater. But that afternoon he found himself in line in that place waiting to order something that was bound to have some preservatives in it and to be served with white bread.

As he walked into the dining-room with his tray of food, he noticed two of his students at a table. One of them stood and waved to him to join them.

Before he could touch his food, the student who had invited the teacher to sit at the table asked what his view of happiness was. Evidently, the students had been heatedly discussing the topic with each other. Had he been invited to act as a referee, he wondered.

It turned out that he didn't have to arbitrate an argument. While sharing with the students the Bahá'í view of happiness, without mentioning the Faith, it dawned on him that by going to the students' cafeteria he had been given an opportunity to teach. He was elated, unbothered by the noise and smoke. The students were intrigued, fascinated; they asked penetrating questions, finally insisting that the teacher reveal the source of his philosophy. And he did.

A few weeks later, after more luncheon conversations, one of the students and his wife came to the teacher's home to talk more about the Faith and to pick up Bahá'í literature.

For the teacher, the impulse to do something that opposed a personal dietary commitment was not viewed as a sacrifice but as a bounty and an enlightening experience – enlightening in the sense that he gained some understanding of how vital daily prayer and deepening are to the process known as teaching. Through them we receive a divine shove, sometimes in directions we would rarely venture in otherwise.

FIVE

Why We Teach

In Bahá'u'lláh's Dispensation we are told we are endowed with the capacity to teach. Not to teach is to neglect to develop our human potential, to fail to grow into a complete person, for teaching is a divine gift. 'Of all the gifts of God the greatest is the gift of teaching.'[9]

By teaching we also demonstrate our love for Bahá'u'lláh. Doesn't a lover show his love by pleasing the one he loves?

And by teaching we grow more firm in the Covenant, because we know that firmness in the Covenant means not only embracing the Manifestation of God for this age, but obeying His laws and heeding His exhortations to the best of our ability. So when we teach we grow spiritually stronger, more capable of repulsing sordid or mindless earthly enticements and influences.

We teach, also, to be divinely assisted. Many of us have experienced low points in our lives at one time or another, when nothing seemed to go right, when even our Bahá'í community seemed to be in the doldrums and the Assembly was besieged by a myriad of personal problems of the believers. Then for some reason we begin to teach and the community's spirit soars; even difficult personal situations begin to straighten out. We become optimistic and find the courage and the strength to confront problems we thought insoluble; the community grows more unified, the Assembly is less burdened by interpersonal disputes, and the friends are more loving towards each other and are glad to serve one another. People who aren't Bahá'ís notice the sparkle in the believers' eyes and the glow emanating from Bahá'ís gathered at public meetings, and they are moved to ask what makes the Bahá'ís so happy, and eventually to appear at firesides.

To try to describe how we draw divine assistance to ourselves when we teach is impossible, because a spiritual law is involved. All we know is that cause and effect are operating: teach, and eventually our outlook changes and what once felt like barely coping evolves into contentment.

Meeting the challenge of spiritualizing and uniting the human family is another reason for teaching. We know that the growth of the Faith is due to Bahá'ís arising to share the healing and unifying Message of Bahá'u'lláh. Certainly the world-wide spread of the Faith didn't come about by some precious soul pushing a magical spiritual button and in an instant Bahá'ís resided in more than 1,000 localities. That is the result of teaching.

But through teaching we are also able to help the individual who in his particular way is seeking the truth, a way out of a world of flashing neon messages of instant hope, health and peace of mind, of desperately clashing political ideologies, of hedonism on parade, of superstition-laden religious orders clinging stubbornly to man-made doctrines promoted as divinely revealed. It is this person who, secretly or openly, questions what he was brought up to believe, who shudders at the prevailing confusion within himself and around him, who sincerely yearns for some direction to sanity and to the world of spirituality which seems to elude him whenever he reaches out.

There are so many people like that in the world – many more than we think. Bahá'u'lláh knows their anguish: 'What "oppression" is more grievous than that a soul seeking the truth, and wishing to attain unto the knowledge of God, should know not where to go for it and from whom to seek it?'[10]

A young man from Long Island, New York, was one of the many who was ensnared by the oppression that Bahá'u'lláh describes. He had just returned from the Vietnam War and was appalled to discover that people back home were suffering as he was. They were hollow, frightened creatures, uncertain of the future, unaware of who they really were, searching for something truly to believe in. Everyone seemed to be wandering aimlessly, hoping somehow to find happiness. All of this was going on in a community where people lived in eight- and nine-room houses, had cars, ate well, and where going to college was expected of a high school graduate. The young man observed that in Long Island the people were as oppressed as the Vietnamese. Although the setting was different, the inner pain and longing were the same.

It was madness, he thought. There had to be something better, something more meaningful in life. Certainly what he had experienced in Vietnam and back home was not the reason why humans existed on earth. He was convinced of that.

He launched a quest for truth which dominated his waking hours. He had no career plans; work was for subsisting only.

For five years he searched, investigating Transcendental Meditation, parapsychology and delving into occult studies. He viewed almost every advertisement of a new political school of thought as a possible path to truth – and answered many of them. But the quest seemed to be making little headway. He felt as though he were running in circles, in darkness. He grew more introspective, spending much time alone, meditating in his room or on long walks. Then he started to keep a journal. Almost every day for several years he recorded his feelings and thoughts.

One evening in February 1976, while reading what he had written, it dawned on him when he was about halfway through that he had never once mentioned God. At that point, a passage from the Bible came to mind: 'Ye shall know them by their fruits.'[11]

It was evident to him that the tree was barren. When he reached the last page, he wrote: 'The End. New perspective, new approach.'

At that moment he felt liberated, his mind emptied of the contradictory metaphysical philosophies he had pondered for years; he was in focus, feeling receptive to something new. In a matter of seconds he found himself enveloped by a wonderful white light and a thought came to him, 'You're looking for God.'

With that realization, he knew he had at least found the direction to truth. As the light started to fade, he was aware that he had always been searching for God; but then he wondered, 'What am I to do next, whom do I turn to? Everyone claims they have the way.' Just then the bright loving light returned, embracing him again; and in his mind he heard a voice: 'If the knowledge of God is available, there must be a source.'

Although the light vanished, he remained in a state of joy, a state he had never experienced before. He was certain that he was going to be guided to that source. Two days later he met a Bahá'í who gave him a book to read. Bahá'u'lláh's words seemed to call out to him. There was no doubt in his mind but that his eyes were gazing on the Word of God.

Six years later, a deeply involved Bahá'í, he found himself rereading his journal and was astonished to learn that before he had written the words, 'The End', he had penned a fervent prayer beseeching God to help him. That prayer, which had sprung from the depth of his soul, had been answered almost immediately. All he had had to do was to ask. As he closed the journal, he thought, 'Thank God the Bahá'í gentleman who told me about the Faith wasn't too busy, too tired or too scared to share the Message with me.'

SIX

Training Our Spiritual Selves

Have you ever heard of an Olympic champion runner who didn't train regularly? Or a famous concert violinist who didn't practice daily? Most likely you haven't. It takes more than raw talent to become successful as an athlete, musician, artist or dancer. Conditioning is required. Without it, the performer will falter, regardless of his potential. The same is true of a Bahá'í teacher.

Prayer and deepening are to an effective Bahá'í teacher as calisthenics and daily running are to a 1,500-meters champion, or practice is to a world-class pianist. In order for a Bahá'í to succeed as a teacher, he has to be in good spiritual condition. Developing it depends on personal discipline, something many of us resist because we feel it requires too much effort; it seems to restrict our freedom, and we doubt whether we are capable of doing it, even though we have done it in the past, never thinking that we were exercising discipline.

For example, today we brush our teeth regularly. Though that hygienic practice is done routinely now, there probably was a time when we resisted it, complaining what a waste of time it was. The same was true with washing before eating. Today, not brushing our teeth or washing would be a departure from our life-style that would make us feel uncomfortable.

The same thing can happen with prayer and deepening. Chances are that it will require considerable effort initially to integrate prayer and deepening into our life's daily schedule, but eventually it would be sorely missed, if for some reason we were unable to pray or deepen one day. The day would feel incomplete; we would feel uneasy, more tense than usual.

A Massachusetts man, who had finally arranged his life to include daily prayer and deepening, learned what it was like to break the pattern.

He had just come home from the office. The doorbell rang. It was a university professor arriving to talk to him about the Faith. The two got together every Wednesday at four p.m.

The Bahá'í wasn't in the mood to do anything with people. He wanted to be alone, perhaps sleep. Turning the seeker away, or pretending illness passed through his mind. But he couldn't do that.

They were in the den – alone. Sensing his friend's discomfort, the professor said, 'Is there something wrong? You seem unusually tense.'

The Bahá'í reflected for a moment. It had been a busy day, even in the morning. With all of the phone calls, the children's questions, and last-minute preparation for a work project, he had forgotten to pray and deepen. It took the professor's inquiry to remind the Bahá'í that he had forgotten to do what had grown to be the most important aspect of each day. 'No wonder I feel tense, anxious and irritable', he thought. A smile crossed his face and he said, 'It's amazing what can happen to a person when he forgets to pray and deepen. Had you not sensed my uneasiness and mentioned it to me I would never have discovered why I feel so edgy, so self-centered.'

The two men read some prayers, and went on to discuss the Faith. In a few weeks the professor became a Bahá'í, and the one-time atheist integrated prayer and deepening into his daily life. No doubt what he experienced in his friend's den impressed upon him how vital prayer and deepening are to maintaining sanity and discovering happiness.

Finding the time to pray and deepen seems to be our greatest problem. Maybe if we truly understood the nature of the human being, we would make a determined effort to plan our lives to find the time.

By reading the Writings we have learned that we have two natures – a spiritual or higher nature and a physical or lower one. For them to mature, to develop their capacities to the fullest, they need to be cultivated and nurtured as long as we live.

Living in a society that doesn't give much recognition to our spiritual nature, but gives an inordinate amount of attention to the development of our bodies, it's easy to neglect our spiritual selves. We know what happens to us physically when we don't eat properly, avoid exercise, don't sleep enough: we become more susceptible to disease, we weaken and tire easily, and age more quickly.

Driving God out of our consciousness has a similar effect on us spiritually, except that the deterioration process isn't as discernible. Physical neglect can be detected in a mirror, by a physician, or by other people such as our relatives, friends and fellow workers. But because most of them are generally in a comparable spiritual condition, they can't notice the effects of our spiritual neglect – and life grows more frightening, more uncertain as we quicken our pace in pursuing greater, more pleasurable material comforts, feeling that perhaps through them we will be led to everlasting happiness.

As Bahá'ís we recognize our spiritual nature and are faced with the challenge of developing it. The more we grow spiritually, the more committed we are to our involvement in the growth process. But for most of us, getting started is difficult. There are many material distractions, some of which have already been mentioned. Perhaps for the Western believer, employing a systematic approach would help him to start and sustain the development of his spiritual nature, since he is already engaged in such an approach in the development of his physical nature.

His eating schedule is a prime example. He usually eats breakfast at a certain time, eats something during the coffee break two hours later, consumes more food at lunch. There's more to eat at the afternoon coffee break. After supper, the daily cycle is completed with a pre-bedtime snack. For practically 365 days a year he follows the same eating pattern. Deviating from it is rare. When it occurs, he may grumble, become irritable or uncommunicative. So he makes sure he maintains the system.

Although we know it is important to seek balance in our lives – and that means developing both of our natures – in the long run our spiritual nature is more important to us, for there will come a time when our physical nature disintegrates and we are left in the world of the spirit for eternity.

A System of Spiritual Development

How can we systematize the development of our spiritual nature? We are fortunate that we don't have to ponder what we must do or, to some extent, when it should be done. Bahá'u'lláh provides us with that information. Without it, creating a productive system would invariably lead to frustration and abandonment of the project.

Consider what Bahá'u'lláh asks us to do in order to grow spiritually. We must say an obligatory prayer daily. Which one of the three He gave us? He leaves that for us to choose. He requires us to read from the Creative Word in the morning and in the evening – and to meditate on it. Bringing ourselves into account daily is urged. Bahá'u'lláh also asks us to recite the Greatest Name ninety-five times some time during the day. There is no one approved way of integrating that guidance into a system. That is left for the believer to decide.

One American worked out a system of spiritual development for himself based on his personality, nature and understanding of the Teachings. It not only helped him to grow but provided him with a sharper focus in identifying and solving his problems and in dealing with the world in general. He's more secure, confident, optimistic, caring, happy to serve others and is developing a teaching state of mind.

When he gets up in the morning, he has his spiritual breakfast before his material breakfast. Of course, others might want to do it the other way around.

Before meeting his Lord in prayer, he washes his hands and face, as Bahá'u'lláh prescribes; then goes to a special spot in the house where he won't be disturbed. Creating a spiritual hideout is also prompted by a recommendation from Bahá'u'lláh, that we recite 'the verses revealed by God' 'in the privacy of [our] chamber'.[12]

After praying, which includes saying the long obligatory prayer, he deepens himself by reading a page or paragraph, sometimes a sentence from the Writings of Bahá'u'lláh or 'Abdu'l-Bahá – and meditates on what he's read. The prayers and deepening usually take about twenty minutes. Rarely much longer, because he's taken to heart Bahá'u'lláh's teaching that prayer should refresh, not tire, the soul.

He goes to work after eating breakfast, fortified to face a world that doesn't operate on a spiritual level. Two hours later, at the office, the coffee cart comes by with a hefty stock of pastries and doughnuts. It's coffee break time. He purchases something to drink and, at times, a doughnut or cheese pastry, but he spends half of the fifteen-minute break alone, reciting the Greatest Name ninety-five times. And he needs to do that, because despite his early morning session with God, he's been exposed to backbiting, gossip, lying, cheating, office politics, discourtesy, insensitivity and rudeness. With spiritual refortification, he's able to meet more worldly challenges. To make sure he gets through the day, he looks for an opportunity to share the Message, directly or indirectly, with someone during lunchtime. During the afternoon coffee break, he recites the Remover of Difficulties for however long he feels it is necessary.

About half an hour before going to sleep, he retreats to his special spot in the house where he'll bring himself to account, evaluating his day, thinking of how he could have done things better, how he could have been a more effective human being. At times he'll look into the

Writings for guidance on how to correct his mistakes or improve his attitude. Then he'll pray and deepen, going to sleep with his mind focused on the soul-purifying words of Bahá'u'lláh and 'Abdu'l-Bahá.

For several years he's been able to maintain the system even during his extensive travels. Obviously, adjustments are made when away from home. For example, if he must share a room with someone, he'll make sure to get up thirty minutes before his roommate. If it is dark, he'll recite those prayers he has committed to memory, and meditate on those passages he knows by heart. At times he'll leave the room and find a spot elsewhere, as he did when he attended a Bahá'í conference in Panama, where he slept with fifty others in a dormitory on the edge of a jungle. He had to go outside to pray and deepen and did the same thing before going to bed. Actually, it wasn't an original idea, because he found others rapt in prayer when he stepped onto the lawn.

Although it was difficult to start the system, mainly because he had never done anything like it before, the more he did it, the easier it was to do, until it was totally integrated into his life's daily routine. The system of developing his spiritual nature became as necessary to him as meeting his daily food requirements. And he learned that it took less time to nurture his spiritual nature every day than to eat breakfast, lunch, supper and the two coffee breaks – about an hour altogether. But more important, he's making progress in attaining the condition that Bahá'u'lláh describes in one of His prayers for protection: 'Armed with the power of Thy name nothing can ever hurt me, and with Thy love in my heart all the world's afflictions can in no wise alarm me.'[13]

Some sacrifice is required in adopting the system,

sacrifice in terms of giving up some time normally devoted to material pursuits such as sleeping and watching television. What it really calls for is the re-structuring of our life's daily schedule. Nothing drastic. But to someone who isn't accustomed to changing his pattern of life, there may be resistance or hesitancy in becoming involved in the process of spiritual development. Fear of failure could be a factor; fear of upsetting a secure routine may be another.

Those who are moved to take the step will find themselves waking earlier in the morning, about twenty to thirty minutes earlier. Undoubtedly some of the starters might be plagued by twinges of self-pity, thinking about the sleep they've given up, and wondering if the effort is worth it. It takes raw faith to believe that waking up earlier to pray and deepen will eventually leave you far more refreshed than sleeping a half-hour later in the morning.

Only those involved in the process can appreciate what it provides the participants. Attempts can be made to describe the feeling, the attitude, the outlook that you eventually attain, but you have to experience the growth process to appreciate the results.

One thing becomes apparent – you possess more energy than ever before to serve the Cause, particularly as a teacher. And it doesn't matter how old you are, or how strange you seem outwardly, the energy derived from cultivating your spiritual nature equips you with a magnetism that can only come from a source beyond the earthly plane. A New York seeker encountered such a person; and it helped to change the direction of his life.

The Effect of a Developed Spiritual Nature

He was asked by a Bahá'í friend to attend a fireside at Vaffa Kinney's apartment in mid-Manhattan. Although he was enamored with the Faith, he had never heard of the woman who had been described to him as an outstanding Bahá'í, someone who had met and served the Master.

She didn't come to the door when they rang the bell. Instead they were greeted by a tall, blond, beaming young man, and four dogs – all different sizes and colors and yelping lovingly. The seeker thought, 'I know Bahá'ís believe in the oneness of humankind, but do they also believe in the oneness of dogdom?'

After being greeted warmly by the young man and dogs, they were ushered into the foyer, and the seeker was startled again. Birds – a rich variety of them – flapped overhead. Some non-human creature was screeching in the parlor. (The seeker later learned it was a big, black, beautiful raven perched on the window sill.) Nervous, because he had never been to a place like that before, the seeker's stomach grew unsettled. He needed to use the bathroom.

While locking the door to the narrow room, he wondered if what he had just experienced was real. Then he heard a strange, squealing sound from behind the shower curtain. He froze. 'Maybe the sound is coming from a leaky shower head', he thought. Suddenly, the curtain parted and out jumped a monkey in a red dress, extending its hand to the seeker. He surprised himself. Instead of bolting from the room, he took the monkey's hand in his own, calmly unlocked the door and stepped into the foyer.

The famous Vaffa Kinney was standing there, regal, with black hair, obviously dyed, for she was in her mid-seventies at the time. Her gaunt face, dominated by an aquiline nose, was tilted heavenwards, a mannerism associated with New York City's aristocracy. The black beads that hung from her neck to her knees overshadowed her long green flower-patterned dress. What impressed the seeker was that she wasn't flustered by the odd couple before her. She viewed it as perfectly natural. In fact, she seemed pleased to see the tall soldier holding the hand of the monkey. 'So you found Suzy!' she exclaimed in a high-pitched voice.

The penthouse apartment was packed with a varied assortment of people, people who normally wouldn't associate with one another. Elegantly dressed men and women fraternized with humble shopkeepers and men from the Bowery (New York's skid row) in tattered clothes with fresh scabs on their faces and hands. The seeker had never seen that kind of human association before. He had been to other firesides and had witnessed the harmony between blacks and whites and Christians and Jews, but being at the Kinney home was like being in a different world. What some noted social scientists claimed couldn't happen was happening. People with extreme differences were genuinely communicating with one another. What he was involved in was no dramatic stage performance or dream. The young man was moved, because as long as he could remember he had hoped one day to discover evidence that the establishment of world brotherhood was possible. Before encountering the Bahá'ís he had been losing hope. What he experienced at the Kinney home convinced him that there was a good chance that his greatest wish could be realized. It didn't matter that the raven was chattering, the dogs were running back and forth, birds were gliding overhead and a monkey in a red dress was prancing about. The spirit in the Kinney home lifted everyone out of the material realm. Those who were there felt at ease, at peace. That apartment, to the seeker, was a capsule containing a promise fulfilled – the Kingdom of Heaven was on Earth.

A dignified black woman, Vereda Pearson, sat down at the piano and played several chords. The talking stopped. The birds retreated to their resting places; the raven became quiet; Suzy the monkey sat on the floor and leaned against the wall; the dogs lay down next to each other. 'An incredible scene', the seeker thought.

Mrs Kinney stood before the fifty or sixty people seated there, most of them in the six or seven rows of wooden folding chairs in the middle of her parlor. She stood straight, brimming with confidence. It was a confidence that had nothing to do with her ability as a speaker, because she wasn't a gifted speaker. Her confidence stemmed from obedience to the Master. He told her once that when speaking she should consider her audience like beautiful birds waiting to hear a wonderful melody, and herself like an organ played by invisible hands, and to be sure to take that attitude because she was alive with the breath of the Holy Spirit.

The seeker, who became a Bahá'í several months after attending Vaffa Kinney's fireside, now understands why she stood in silence a few moments before addressing the audience. She was getting herself out of the way so that she could become a clear channel for the Holy Spirit. Exuding devotion to God's Cause, she greeted everyone warmly and introduced Edward Schlesinger, the speaker.

Though in the background, Vaffa Kinney was involved every second during Mr Schlesinger's brilliant talk. She was seated behind him, praying. Years later, he confided to friends that whenever he spoke at Mrs Kinney's fireside, he could never recall what he said there.

Because of Vaffa Kinney's fireside, many people became Bahá'ís: socialists, atheists, Orthodox Jews, vegetarians, feminists, Hindus and conventional types – those who would generally try to avoid attending a meeting in such an odd setting and who would be more comfortable seated in a pew of a Presbyterian or Episcopalian church. They all came, and so attracted were they to the loving spirit in the Kinney home that the animals and strange-looking people didn't bother them very much. In fact, after a while even the most conventional seeker began to appreciate, even enjoy, the atmosphere, no longer considering it strange but, rather, unique. It was through Mrs Kinney's fireside that a conservative gentleman, who later became a leading New York real estate executive, became a Bahá'í.

Mrs Kinney longed to pioneer. But every appeal to the Guardian to leave New York was turned down. Finally, at the age of seventy-five, she was granted permission. Mrs Kinney didn't go far; but to her, a native New Yorker, moving across the Hudson River was like moving to another world. In a matter of weeks, she was holding firesides in her new home in River Edge, New Jersey. Soon seekers appeared and a number of them accepted Bahá'u'lláh.

Vaffa Kinney was an outstanding teacher because she was prepared to teach. By daily involvement in developing her spiritual nature, she became a mighty spiritual magnet. A pure heart couldn't resist her. She was teaching all the time, because it was part of her consciousness. For her, there was no special time to teach – every moment was devoted to teaching. She didn't live to teach; she taught to live.

At times she would call her son very early in the morning when he was asleep. It wasn't a call of desperation, but rather an expression of amazement, a desire to share a new meaning she had gained from a passage she had probably read hundreds of times. Until the day she passed away, Vaffa Kinney was involved in the process of nurturing her spiritual nature. She outstandingly exemplified the idea that teaching is a state of mind.

SEVEN

Attaining a Prayerful Condition

Many of us know what it's like to be over-eager in sharing Bahá'u'lláh's Message with others. At the time we were so full of enthusiasm, we weren't aware of offending anyone. The desire to teach was so intense that we didn't even pray before approaching a seeker. Now we know why our overture was greeted indifferently or rejected.

For most of us, wisdom comes gradually. From experience, we have learned that effort is required to attain it. The more we grow, the more sensitive we become in our communication with others, and the more effective we are as teachers.

Prayer is one of the most important steps in our climb toward wisdom. Without it, we rely on our own will and human instincts; and we know where that can lead us.

The very act of prayer is acknowledgement of our poverty, our ignorance, and our weakness, and of God's wealth, knowledge and power. So we reach out to Him for direction. 'Abdu'l-Bahá explains what happens to a believer when he does this: ' . . . this supplication is by itself a light to his heart, an illumination to his sight, a life to his soul and an exaltation to his being.'[14]

Trying to teach without prayer is like trying to drive an automobile without fuel. Through will power we might be able to push a car, but not for long, and certainly not very far. Just as fuel is needed to spark the engine, prayer helps to generate the desire to share the Word of God. Resorting only to hurried supplication moments before engaging in a teaching event is much like stroking a rabbit's foot for luck. The ideal is to attain a prayerful condition.[15] In that condition one understands that God is the source of all life, and that through regular prayer we develop ourselves as channels for His guidance which flows through us, and we say and do the right thing. It seems mechanistic, but it's not. To some people, praying is equated with pressing a vending-machine button to obtain a product. There is a basic difference. It is true that in prayer we beseech and ask, and that could be construed figuratively as pushing a button, albeit a spiritual button. But unlike purchasing a soft drink from a vending machine, we don't anticipate God's response. Whatever He provides is viewed as right for us, even if at the time it doesn't appear that it is what we need. Someone in a prayerful condition will accept God's guidance regardless of what it is, realizing that in time the wisdom of the Divine response will become clear. Because he doesn't anticipate what form the celestial communication will take, he is in a perpetual state of wonderment, looking forward eagerly to what God has in store for him. No wonder Bahá'u'lláh says, 'Increase my wonderment and amazement at Thee, O God!'[16]

Though for most of us attaining a prayerful condition takes time, often considerable time, to wait until we reach our goal before teaching would be a mistake. By adopting such an attitude we'll certainly fail to achieve a prayerful condition. This is because, as has been stated earlier, divine assistance is cut off if we don't teach. Without such help we are not inclined to pray. So instead of growing spiritually, we find ourselves drifting into that part of the world we know is decaying – and there probably isn't a more painful conflict.

Those who have attained a prayerful condition wouldn't say so, for humility is an essential element of that condition. God certainly knows who they are. No worldly prerequisites are required to reach such a state. Every human being can attain it, even those whom, in our weaker moments, we consider crude, backward and lacking good character. Those who have attained a prayerful condition come from all walks of life, but they have one thing in common: they have taken to heart Bahá'u'lláh's appeal to His followers: 'They should put their trust in God, and, holding fast unto Him, follow in His way. Then will they be made worthy of the effulgent glories of the sun of divine knowledge and understanding, and become the recipients of a grace that is infinite and unseen . . .'[17]

Those blessed with a prayerful attitude turn to God first when confronted with a crisis, a problem, a decision in any aspect of life, whether it be at work, school, or dealing with family matters. But they hadn't always done this. It took effort, consistent effort, much spiritual stumbling and many heart-wrenching tests, before turning to God first became automatic.

Curtis Kelsey was such a man. Poorly educated – in fact he never finished elementary school – he grew in wisdom because he tried to rely first on God in all matters, even intimate family issues. The stronger his reliance grew, the more opportunities he was given to share the Faith, especially among the highly educated. That was a test for him, because he was always aware of his lack of formal schooling. But how could he shrink from proclaiming the Faith?

When sitting next to Curtis, who was the speaker at a public meeting, a young believer sensed he was near someone who had attained a prayerful condition. It became apparent when he noticed Curtis's lips moving slightly. Curtis wasn't rehearsing his speech, because his eyes were fixed on a realm that was beyond the obvious. He was reciting the Greatest Name, and continued to recite it throughout the long introduction given him. Curtis strode to the podium consumed by the love of God.

Those who are in a prayerful condition know that they are not the cause of attracting someone to the Faith; they are simply a vehicle for the Holy Spirit that penetrates a seeker's heart and moves him into Bahá'u'lláh's out-stretched arms. Obviously it takes strong faith to leave all of our affairs in God's hands and believe that He is truly our guide and refuge. Without prayer we can't realize such an understanding nor experience the exhilaration and excitement of being a channel for the Holy Spirit.

Those who were at the Green Acre school one evening to hear Curtis Kelsey speak sensed that he was guided by a divine force. Some of the words that passed from his lips surprised even himself. This became evident to all after he had made a certain point in his talk; he laughed and exclaimed, 'That's a great idea!' referring to what he had just said. He shook his head in amazement and laughed again.

In most societies people have a stereotyped image of

what someone in a prayerful condition looks like and how he behaves. That image was dashed for a New Jersey delegate to a United States National Bahá'í Convention in the mid-1960s. A Hand of the Cause from Canada approached the podium, dressed in a navy blue suit, looking very much like a business executive, which he was. When he started talking about prayer, emphasizing the long obligatory prayer, the believer was startled. 'What that man is saying', the delegate thought, 'should be coming from someone whose hair is longer and who isn't wearing a tie.' He had chosen the short obligatory prayer for himself, because he felt it was more in keeping with his culture. The long one was for orientals who were accustomed to genuflecting, placing their foreheads on the ground. It was something he believed he could never do. But what the Hand of the Cause was saying was penetrating his heart. His attitude was changing not only because of the speaker's genuineness and love for everyone in the audience. He was also moved by the fact that someone whom he could easily relate to – a successful North American professional – was committed to something that appeared so alien. When the Hand of the Cause shared what he and others had experienced from saying the long obligatory prayer, the delegate was inspired to try it.

To this day he says it, knowing that by placing his forehead on the ground as an expression of his love and reverence for God and Bahá'u'lláh, he grows freer and stronger, more humble and more capable of functioning in a forthright and principled manner within the business world.

As we struggle to attain a prayerful condition, we experience, from time to time, the power of prayer. The unexpected happens. For some of us, miracles occur. Problems we felt were insoluble are solved. And every time that happens our faith grows, and it becomes easier to pray until we long to do it and every breath becomes a prayer.

The Power of Prayer

A Western Massachusetts woman experienced the power of prayer, and it changed her life – and her family's. When she heard of the Faith, she enthusiastically shared her joy with her husband. But his response was explosive: 'I don't want you going to those meetings with those queer people. I'm a Catholic, my folks are Catholics. People all over town know we are Catholics. You'll disgrace our name if you continue to be with those Bahá'ís.' He paused, his face reddening with rage. 'If you persist in getting together with them, I'll divorce you, and you'll never see the children again.'

A few days later she met a Bahá'í friend in the street and explained her husband's reaction. The Bahá'í advised her to heed her husband's wishes for the sake of family unity. 'But pray for him', she counseled. 'Pray that his heart softens and that he be able to see what the Faith really is.'

She followed this advice. About two weeks later, her husband woke up in the middle of the night, nudged his wife out of a deep sleep and said, 'You know, it's okay to see those Bahá'ís.'

In less than two months, he asked to read a Bahá'í book. He was soon going to firesides. Today both are members of the town's Local Spiritual Assembly.

It isn't always that easy. Another woman prayed for

about thirty years before her husband became a Bahá'í. We can speculate why it took so long, but only God knows why. All we can do is what Bahá'u'lláh urges us to do – and do it with sincerity. Bahá'u'lláh is specific about that in His Tablet of Aḥmad: 'By God! Should one who is in affliction or grief read this Tablet with absolute sincerity, God will dispel his sadness, solve his difficulties and remove his afflictions.'[18]

Only God can judge who is sincere in prayer. But there are obstacles that most of us have experienced that have prevented us from attaining sincerity in our supplications. For example, it might have been our enthusiasm to accomplish a crucial task that drove us to try to bargain with God, finding ourselves thinking something like this: 'Oh, God! If you help me to secure this job promotion, I'll start holding firesides every week.' Not that bargaining with God should be condoned, but at least it is an admission of God's greatness, that ultimately He is in control of everything. It's not an act of willfulness, which springs from the ego. By insisting that God fulfill our desire, we challenge God's authority and question His wisdom. Usually when we resort to demanding that God do our bidding, we are demonstrating our lack of understanding of what our relationship with God should be. But there are times when even though we are aware of God's station, we insist, out of desperation, that God carry out our wish. The order is usually issued when we witness, or are the target of, a great injustice. It is more like a child running to a parent with an appeal that action be taken to correct a wrong committed against him or a friend. Certainly God knows our motives, even our subconscious drives, which are not clear to us; and what may be construed as a demand of God by someone may not be viewed that way by God at all. Of course, if we are headstrong and persist in insisting that God heed our wishes, then what we anticipate won't materialize. God will respond with what He feels we need, and that might come in the form of a test or two.

There is nothing wrong in asking God for something. But once the request is made, there is no need to push it. By doing that we limit God; we act as if He is hard of hearing or doesn't really understand what we want, when in fact He knows our thoughts before they are formulated. This doesn't mean that we shouldn't repeat our requests. What matters is how we make the request.

The ideal attitude is to let go of the message we file with God, and await His response, believing that whatever it may be will be right. A Massachusetts woman, who is working at maintaining such an attitude, took a problem to God. As she viewed it, it was really her Bahá'í community's problem. She was aware of the importance of every Bahá'í community having a diverse membership. Racially and ethnically the community seemed healthy; and there was adequate economic diversity. What was lacking, she felt, was the presence of elderly people. She launched a personal prayer campaign. About a week after she started, she received a telephone call from a local resident who was in her mid-seventies. The woman told the Bahá'í that she had wanted to call her two years earlier after reading about her husband in a local newspaper, but she hadn't had the courage to telephone. 'But,' she said, 'the strangest thing happened. For some reason this week I was able to muster the courage to call you people.' Two weeks later she attended her first fireside. The Bahá'í was delighted but not amazed, because she had had similar experiences. In making her request she had been sincere, hadn't insisted on having her way; she would have been content with whatever God decided to do in responding to her prayers. But she wasn't always so acquiescent. There were still times when she found some answers to her prayers, especially on personal matters, difficult to understand and downright painful. In fact, there were times when her immediate impression was that God was thwarting her efforts and she contemplated ignoring the guidance she had received. Fortunately, her willingness to know and obey the Divine Will was greater than her emotional reaction. She stood firm, but not without the agony that comes from internal conflict. That kind of strength developed only after years of praying regularly, even when she failed to stand firm. God is forgiving and is aware of our efforts, even those we feel are feeble. What is important is that we keep trying. In the end, isn't that what matters most?

Turning to God First

None of us is perfect. Though as Bahá'ís we find ourselves on the pathway to perfection, being a Bahá'í doesn't provide automatic forward movement. Progress is dependent on the degree of our reliance on God.

But praying isn't always easy, especially if we feel unworthy of communing with God because we feel guilty about our lack of involvement in the Faith, or because of some of the things we have done that fall short of exemplary Bahá'í behavior. 'He must be disappointed in me', we think – and fear facing Him. But God is All-Merciful and aware of our imperfections, and of the effort needed to progress spiritually, especially during these days when materialism pervades every aspect of life, including religion. To turn our backs on God because we feel unworthy of receiving His help could put us in a tailspin towards destruction, intensifying our sense of guilt along the way. We are human, and are going to make mistakes. But the number of mistakes and indiscretions will diminish as we proceed along the pathway. The more progress we make, the more capable we'll be in facing and learning from our tests. And eventually we'll realize that the greatest mistake is to stop relying on God no matter how severe life may seem, no matter how inadequate we feel, no matter how low we think we are spiritually. By continually reaching out to God, regardless of our situation or state of mind, our dependency on Him will grow – and we'll understand, as the wise ones do, that God is the first one we turn to.

Today a Bahá'í in Fort Worth, Texas knows that; but that realization didn't come easily. There was a time in her life when she was besieged by problems. Financially, the family was in trouble; the children were ill; termites had invaded the house; and Bahá'í teaching was sluggish. She was saying the Tablet of Aḥmad three times a day.

God's response was not what she expected. At two a.m. the telephone rang, waking her up. It was a woman she had been teaching for about nine months, taking her to firesides, potlucks, prayer sessions and social affairs, and listening patiently to her problems. The woman was desperate, begging the Bahá'í to pray for her sick parrot.

After the woman hung up, the Bahá'í was incensed. 'It isn't fair', she said to herself, 'for me to pray for that wealthy woman's dumb bird when my family and I are under so much pressure. Where is the justice?' Furious, she couldn't go back to sleep. Feelings of anger and self-pity meshed and for a while she couldn't think clearly. Finally, she reached out for help and soon she found herself praying for the seeker's parrot.

A few days later the woman called back, thanking the Bahá'í for her prayers. Her parrot had been healed. Following the conversation, the Bahá'í unleashed her anger, asking why the bird was helped and she and her family remained in the same sorry situation. To the Bahá'í there seemed to be no divine response to her feelings. In the meantime, the bird fell ill at least four more times and the Bahá'í was requested each time to say special prayers. The parrot recovered every time.

After the Bahá'í realized the humor of the parrot episode, her personal situation improved and the bird's owner became a dedicated servant of Bahá'u'lláh.

Approaches to Prayer

To resort to prayer in the face of disappointment, as the Fort Worth woman did, requires a belief that God answers prayers, an ability to discern the guidance He gives and to accept it, certain that it is right. Not everyone can do the latter, especially those of us from an atheistic or agnostic background; even some who pray ardently have trouble. Undoubtedly some have learned through experience and a period of trial and error and tests; but there are also sincere souls who are unable to distinguish a divine sign from the multitude of events they are exposed to daily. For them, and for everyone else, there are various approaches to prayer, one of which was shared by the Guardian with an American believer, Ruth Moffett, while she was on pilgrimage. He stated there were five steps that could be taken when approaching God with a problem or wishing for His help:

First Step – Pray and meditate about it. Use the prayers of the manifestations as they have the greatest power. Then remain in the silence of contemplation for a few minutes.

Second Step – Arrive at a decision and hold this. This decision is usually born during the contemplation. It may seem almost impossible of accomplishment but if it seems to be as answer to a prayer or a way of solving the problem, then immediately take the next step.

Third Step – Have determination to carry the decision through. Many fail here. The decision, budding into determination, is blighted and instead becomes a wish or a vague longing. When determination is born, immediately take the next step.

Fourth Step – Have faith and confidence that the power will flow through you, the right way will appear, the door will open, the right thought, the right message, the right principle or the right book will be given you. Have confidence, and the right thing will come to your need. Then, as you rise from prayer, take at once the fifth step.

Fifth Step – Then, he said, lastly, ACT; Act as though it had all been answered. Then act with tireless, ceaseless energy. And as you act, you, yourself, will become a magnet, which will attract more power to your being, until you become an unobstructed channel for the Divine power to flow through you. Many pray but do not remain for the last half of the first step. Some who meditate arrive at a decision, but fail to hold it. Few have the determination to carry the decision through, still fewer have the confidence that the right thing will come to their need. But how many remember to act as though it had all been answered? How true are those words – 'Greater than the prayer is the spirit in which it is uttered' and greater than the way it is uttered is the spirit in which it is carried out.[19]

EIGHT

The Importance of Deepening

An American Auxiliary Board member received an appeal one night from a District Teaching Committee within his area of service, asking for new teaching techniques. Though eager to teach, the committee spokesman seemed frustrated. Everything they had tried, he said, had produced poor results. What the committee was looking for, the Auxiliary Board member sensed, was something magical, a gimmick – something he couldn't produce.

He made a date to meet with them anyway, wondering how he could help those valiant souls who were in the field trying to coordinate a district-wide teaching effort in the midst of apathy, insensitivity and a concern for worldly pursuits. They were a heroic group, wanting the Faith to grow more than anything else.

He certainly didn't want to disappoint them; but he was afraid that he would, because he couldn't provide them with what they wanted. Nevertheless, in his eagerness to help, he tried to think of special techniques and devices. Nothing emerged because intuitively he felt that trying to concoct some contrived scheme was alien to the spirit of the Faith; it didn't seem right. He prayed, and the response came in the form of a thought: share with the friends the way prayer and deepening improve our teaching effort. There was no doubt in his mind that this was what the committee needed to understand; but convincing them would be difficult. In fact, he was afraid that it would alienate them, because they had heard him talk about it before, not once but several times, at institutes, conferences, even at the District Convention. They wanted something that would guarantee quick and fantastic results, not more words and inspirational stories.

Through meditation he conceived of a new approach in sharing the same message – and prayed for protection and assistance, because he didn't want to discourage or offend them. He truly wanted to serve them. In his heart he knew that by integrating prayer and deepening as a part of their daily schedule the teaching state of mind would eventually evolve. He knew it from personal experience. But he was having trouble communicating, because the committee was bent on gaining access to some special wonder method.

'If they would only try what I suggest,' he thought, during some moments of frustration, 'they would obtain the results they are looking for. After all, what I've been sharing with them is not something I've invented. It is something Bahá'u'lláh, 'Abdu'l-Bahá, Shoghi Effendi and now the Universal House of Justice urge us to do.'

With some trepidation he drove off to meet the committee, praying that this time he would be able to reach their hearts.

At the meeting, he shared what he had carefully prepared, but he sensed that it wasn't penetrating. They were tolerating him, trying hard to be courteous. From the looks on their faces they seemed to be saying to themselves: 'I've heard this stuff before; the same old rehash.'

When there was no response to his invitation to ask questions, he sat back feeling that he had failed again. Then the door bell rang. In walked a slender young lady. She wasn't quite five feet tall and appeared fragile, someone you wouldn't want to greet with a slap on the back for fear she would collapse.

When she was introduced as an area representative of the committee, the secretary leaned toward the Auxiliary Board member and whispered: 'She holds the most successful fireside in the District. More than ten people have become Bahá'ís through it. And she's able to attract people others have written off as unteachable.'

Impressed, he focused his attention on her. 'My God!' he thought. 'She seems so shy, so bird-like.' He waited for her to say something, but she didn't utter a word for some time, preferring to listen.

While the committee reviewed the conditions of several promising groups, he wondered what made her such an effective teacher. When the thought of asking her if she deepened every day flashed through his mind, he grew anxious. 'It would be great', he thought, 'if she would reveal that she did. Then the committee would have living proof that what I've been suggesting works.' But he hesitated, because he didn't want to embarrass her. He knew what it was like to be put on the spot. After all, deepening is such a personal matter.

'Why not ask her?' a voice from within ordered.

Her eyes lit up and she smiled when the question was raised. 'Oh, yes', she exclaimed with assurance. 'I read the Writings every morning and evening.' And then she asked very innocently, 'Isn't that what we are supposed to do as Bahá'ís?'

'Does deepening help your teaching effort?' he inquired.

'It gives me energy, focus, makes me happy and gives me the desire to teach.'

The Auxiliary Board member leaned back on the couch and silently thanked Bahá'u'lláh for guiding the area representative to the meeting. He could tell that the committee, already impressed with her teaching results, now understood the reason for her success.

If trying to teach without prayer is like trying to drive an automobile without fuel, trying to share the Message without deepening is like trying to drive with a faulty battery. We don't get very far, and driving becomes a terrible nuisance. Eventually we don't want to drive at all.

Deepening can be likened to recharging the battery. Deepen daily and our spiritual energy grows. When that happens, we see the necessity for teaching, we develop a desire to teach; but more important, we gain a real appreciation for deepening as the mainspring of spiritual energy. As we continue to deepen, it will become apparent to us how important it is to include deepening in our daily routine. That realization will have been born from experience; for we will have felt the power that springs from the Creative Word surging in our hearts, making us more alert, more conscious of others' needs and concerns, more kindly, more loving, more desirous of wanting to help others. To be cut off from that power becomes our greatest fear. Isn't that, in part, what is meant by the fear of God?

The Example of George Spendlove

Certainly George Spendlove was aware of the need to deepen. The Canadian scholar and museum curator wasn't timid about sharing his feelings about the matter, especially at Bahá'í schools like Green Acre in Eliot, Maine. But there were some in the audience who considered his statements on deepening dogmatic; and those who felt that way were puzzled that such a respected intellectual could be so emphatic, so certain about things. Sharing this view was a relatively new Bahá'í, proud of his university training and academic attainments. Had he not been with his wife of two months, he would have walked out of Mr Spendlove's first lecture. It didn't matter that almost everyone else, including his wife, seemed spellbound by what the man was saying.

Mr Spendlove's odd manner and deliberate speech heightened the young Bahá'í's feelings. Sitting before the new Bahá'í and about forty other people was this man of about fifty-five, who appeared older, not only because he was bald and wore a hearing aid, but because he was contemplative, resembling a venerable oriental monk. He seemed to ooze wisdom, especially when he spoke with his eyes closed. The infuriated young Bahá'í was repelled by the sight, because he felt Mr Spendlove was staging a performance. Of course, at the time the young man wasn't aware that this strange speaking manner was the result of wounds sustained in World War One.

What disturbed him most was a statement that he felt, at the time, was outrageous. It dealt with Bahá'u'lláh's appeal to His followers to read from the Creative Word every morning and evening. He squirmed in his seat after hearing Mr Spendlove exclaim with great certitude and long pauses between phrases: 'If one evening your house were on fire and you hadn't read from the Creative Word, you would be better off, in the long run, to remain in the house and read than immediately to race outside.'

'Absurd', the young man thought. And he thought of at least five ways of achieving the same end without becoming consumed by an inferno.

Over the years the young man matured, finally grasping that statement. He grew to love George Spendlove, not only because of his wit and sweetness, but because he was a mountain jutting out of a wild sea. He learned where this remarkable man drew his strength. And in later years, whenever he thought of George Spendlove, walking across an open field or sharing his thoughts with others on the porch of Green Acre's inn, a certain Hidden Word would come to mind:

O My Brother! Hearken to the delightsome words of My honeyed tongue, and quaff the stream of mystic holiness from My sugar-shedding lips. Sow the seeds of My divine wisdom in the pure soil of thy heart, and water them with the water of certitude, that the hyacinths of My knowledge and wisdom may spring up fresh and green in the sacred city of thy heart.[20]

The Nature of Deepening

Deepening isn't a complicated process. It's like growing a flower. With the proper amount of water, sunlight and cultivation, the seed blossoms into what it is intended to be. In a sense, reading from the Creative Word and meditating on what we read are to us what water and sunlight are to a plant. Without essential care the flower wilts. Without partaking of the soul-enriching water, that is the divine verses, we shrivel up spiritually.

As many of us already realize, reading prayers alone isn't deepening, although it's most helpful to have a prayerful attitude when deepening. Two of the basic steps of deepening are reading and meditating on the Writings of Bahá'u'lláh and 'Abdu'l-Bahá, as well as the writings of the Guardian and the Universal House of Justice.

Deepening implies immersion. We can be aware of something, but not really appreciate it. It is like the perspiring man standing on the shore of a lake at high noon on a blistering hot day, seeking relief. He is aware of the body of water, but will appreciate it only when he plunges into it.

Bahá'u'lláh invites us to plunge into His Revelation, knowing how much it will benefit us: 'Immerse yourselves in the ocean of My words, that ye may unravel its secrets, and discover all the pearls of wisdom that lie hid in its depths.'[21]

To be engaged in true deepening we need to understand as well as know the Teachings. It is possible to know a great deal and understand very little. For example: had the man on the lake's shore refused to enter the water, he might have been able to describe the size, shape, and color of the lake but wouldn't have been able to describe how it felt.

It is understanding that generates feelings of enthusiasm, wonderment and security. Without them, we can't teach effectively. Evidence of the importance of understanding the Teachings can be found throughout the Sacred Text. The word 'understanding' usually follows the words 'know' or 'knowledge'. There is an implied distinction between knowing and understanding that often eludes us. Understanding is more than knowing, though we can't understand if we don't first know.

Meditation

How do we gain understanding? One way – and perhaps the most significant way – is by meditating on what we read, a procedure urged by Bahá'u'lláh: 'Do thou meditate on that which We have revealed unto thee, that thou mayest discover the purpose of God, thy Lord, and the Lord of all worlds.'[22]

Of course the term 'meditation' conjures up in our minds an image of someone sitting in a strange position and chanting something unintelligible. So we avoid meditation, even though unbeknownst to ourselves we sometimes meditate. Oh, it is nothing planned, because it is executed suddenly during a situation that requires deep reflection. That's all that meditation is in the Bahá'í world – deep reflection. It can also be called concentrated thought, deep thinking or spiritual day-dreaming.

Meditation, for most of us, is viewed as a spiritual exercise. Not necessarily, as 'Abdu'l-Bahá points out:

The meditative faculty is akin to the mirror; if you put it before earthly objects it will reflect them. Therefore if the spirit of man is contemplating earthly subjects he will be informed of these.

But if you turn the mirror of your spirits heavenwards . . . the rays of the Sun of Reality will be reflected in your hearts, and the virtues of the Kingdom will be obtained.[23]

In essence, meditating on the Writings is reflective reading. We read, then stop to ponder what we have read. It is the pondering that can produce exciting results.

Meaningful insight or understanding of a passage comes like light breaking through dark clouds. The elation that comes with that discovery sets off a yearning to put into practice what has been discovered, and action is taken. Where there is understanding, there is a genuine desire to do. Simply knowing doesn't spark action. For example, there are many people who know that racial prejudice is an ugly, destructive social force, but do nothing to eradicate it within themselves or in the society in which they live. Their knowledge of race prejudice comes from reading about it or from radio and television. When confronted by it through the media, they express concern for a few moments, but then turn to matters they really feel are more important. There is no incentive for commitment. Through meditation, however, we gain an appreciation of the destructiveness of racism, because we will have thought deeply about it, sometimes so deeply that we are able to sense the frustration, the inner pain that victims of racism have to endure day after day. Action usually follows such an experience, because we have been aroused emotionally, and we want to do something to help. Often the first step taken is in the form of inquiring more about racism so that meaningful measures can be taken to combat the problem. And because meditation reveals so much in the first instance, it is employed again and again, and our understanding of racism continues to grow, generating deeper and deeper involvement.

Imagine what can happen to us as Bahá'ís if through meditation we continue to gain insight or understanding of the Sacred Text. We will grow more detached, dwelling more and more in the world of the spirit. Of course, not as monks, because we know that asceticism is forbidden in the Faith, but as people working like everyone else in the world.

Really, all that deepening involves is reading with care, and that requires thought. Whether it is brilliant or slow thought doesn't matter. What matters most is the effort to reflect on the Creative Word. Then understanding will eventually come. But not always when we expect it. We read and meditate on a passage in the morning, and while driving home from work understanding of that passage unfolds in our mind and whatever tensions we have accumulated during the day vanish – and joy overcomes us, making some of us want to sing.

Sometimes, however, when our minds aren't riddled with family and work problems, when our spirit is truly refreshed, understanding comes quickly, at times coming during meditation itself. For most of us that doesn't happen often, mainly because we don't always approach deepening with a clear mind. A child may be sick, there are unpaid bills, there are the letters that have to be written for the Local Spiritual Assembly, and perhaps five more things that need immediate attention. So enlightenment doesn't come when we deepen. And we fret. Actually, there's no need to fret (more easily said than done), because there will be times when understanding will come. It may be once or twice a month, but that is better than never experiencing it.

Eventually – if we are faithful in deepening regularly – we'll find a way to clear our minds, and we'll gain understanding more often. But even when we reach that stage in our spiritual development, there's no guarantee that enlightenment will come every time we deepen. It's not an automatic process. But it is understandable why we want it to be. After all, experiencing understanding is like giving fuel to the fire of love of God in our hearts; and that gives us more vitality, increases our ardor for teaching, reinforces the spiritual armor that protects us from the assaults of a world going mad.

The Effect of Deepening

An American scientist discovered the value of deepening and prayer after being a Bahá'í for seven years. While at college he had been a radical Marxist, and prayer and deepening weren't as important to him as were Bahá'u'lláh's social teachings. Prayer was for Feasts, he felt, or for opening and closing Assembly meetings. As far as deepening was concerned, he had practically mastered the 'knowing' stage. He knew a great deal, especially about the administration of the Faith and the World Order. The term 'spirituality' mystified him, and he felt uncomfortable discussing it.

Gifted with a keen intellect, zeal and natural organizational ability, he was effective in proclaiming the Faith, and when it came to teaching he was an imaginative creator of techniques.

Two Auxiliary Board members witnessed a demonstration of one of his techniques at an area teaching conference, attended by about sixty believers. The scientist made a dramatic entrance, leading his entourage down the auditorium's center aisle to the stage.

The performance was incredible. Essentially, it was a mock fireside, stressing the do's and don'ts. Though not mentioned, it was obvious that the basis of the approach was a set of behavioral psychological principles: do or say a certain thing and expect a certain response. It was manipulation. But worse than that, the highly acclaimed fireside teaching method allowed for no guidance from the Supreme Concourse. It was a humanistic exercise in the guise of a spiritual approach.

From the audience's standpoint, the method was hailed as a teaching panacea. At last, some stated, we have something that works. The two Auxiliary Board members looked at each other with amazement and concern. They agreed that they should both speak to the scientist, but that it should be done separately, because they didn't want to 'gang up' on him. There was no doubt of the young man's love for Bahá'u'lláh. What had to be done was to redirect his intellect and enthusiasm into a spiritual channel.

When the Covenant of Bahá'u'lláh was mentioned as a source for teaching, the young man seemed puzzled. 'What does the succession of leadership have to do with teaching?' he wondered. He wanted to do the right thing; he certainly didn't want to hurt the Faith in any way. Naturally competitive, he had grown so frustrated by the meager teaching results in his city that he had been driven to devise a 'never-fail' fireside teaching method. But it was obvious to him that the Auxiliary Board members serving in the state where he lived didn't approve of it.

About a month after his first encounter with the Auxiliary Board members, he met them again at a different place. And again they mentioned the importance of relying on the Covenant for teaching. Perplexed, he decided to investigate what the Covenant truly was; and he soon realized that obedience to the Central Figures of the Faith means more than being loyal to them. It also means becoming involved in the process of knowing and understanding their Writings and making them a part of yourself. It became clearer when he discovered this passage from Bahá'u'lláh: 'Recite ye the verses of God every morning and evening. Whoso reciteth them not hath truly failed to fulfill his pledge to the Covenant of God and His Testament . . .'[24]

The next time all three met was under different circumstances. More than 300 Bahá'ís had gathered at a conference sponsored by the young man's Assembly. And he was one of the featured speakers.

When he approached the microphone, many in the audience sensed a spirit emanating from him that comes only from the Supreme Concourse. With tears in his eyes, he said simply: 'I have discovered the Covenant.' The veil to understanding had been lifted from him. Others in the audience, especially his close friends, sensed a change in him.

All sat riveted to their chairs, wondering what he was going to say next. It was something simple. He shared an experience he had had the day after making his discovery. A colleague, he said, from his research lab approached him, asking what had happened to him, for he seemed different in a positive sense. He could respond by saying only what was in his heart, 'I have discovered the Covenant.'

The inquirer didn't flinch, jump back or run away. He was intrigued. More than that. He was attracted to this man he thought he knew – a clever, hard driving, creative chemical researcher brought up in a tough neighborhood in Brooklyn. He asked for an explanation of the Covenant.

Usually confident and articulate, the Bahá'í hesitated for a moment, then tried to describe in a fumbling, rambling manner what the Covenant was. He felt he had failed to communicate. But he was wrong. His colleague's heart had been touched, and that had never happened before when he had been exposed to carefully reasoned and constructed explanations of the Faith. In a few days the colleague became a Bahá'í. As for the one who had discovered the Covenant, he became comfortable with thinking and talking about spirituality. Realizing that firmness in the Covenant was dependent on deepening, he worked out a system for reading and meditating every morning and evening, taking into account this guidance from Bahá'u'lláh:

Recite ye the verses of God in such measure that ye be not overtaken with fatigue or boredom. Burden not your souls so as to cause exhaustion and weigh them down, but rather endeavor to lighten them, that they may soar on the wings of revealed Verses unto the dawning-place of His signs. This is conducive to nearer access unto God, were ye to comprehend. [25]

He decided to deepen for about fifteen minutes each time. At first it was a struggle getting up thirty minutes earlier than usual, but soon he looked forward to being alone with the Creative Word. As he became more dependent on the Teachings in dealing with all aspects of life, his home became a center of Bahá'í activity, a tower of light, attracting all sorts of people, many of whom became Bahá'ís. Through deepening he grew to understand what teaching was and why we teach. The Auxiliary Board member for propagation noticed that teaching had become the 'dominating passion' of the young man's life and asked him to serve as his assistant.

His wife caught the spirit he generated. They held weekly firesides and special dinners for certain seekers every Thursday. This, as well as serving on the Assembly, he as Chairman and she as Secretary. But he had to do more, for there were only six more months left to the Five Year Plan. New localities had to be opened. So on weekends he and a close friend drove 120 miles to the little town they had selected as their locality goal. And they didn't allow the sub-zero temperatures to deter them.

Going to the town week after week wasn't viewed as a hardship. For them it was a party on wheels, an adventure more exciting than a canoeing or camping trip. Even the resistance to the Faith by many of the townspeople didn't discourage them. Using 'Abdu'l-Bahá as an example, they served those whom they met. Because many of the people in town were poor, they collected clothes from the believers in their city and gave them to the town's needy. A local newspaper editor was moved by what the Bahá'ís had done – and inquired about the Faith. In a few months she became a Bahá'í.

Although the young man who had discovered the Covenant was engaged in all this teaching activity, he felt he wasn't doing enough. So he called up the Auxiliary Board member he was assisting to tell him he was quitting his job so that he could devote all of his time to teaching the Faith.

The Auxiliary Board member was flabbergasted. 'I have created a monster', he thought. He loved his assistant, but the young man needed balance and perspective.

It took the Auxiliary Board member twenty minutes to persuade his assistant not to leave his job. Two points helped to change his mind. First, teaching is not a matter of geography; all people need to know about the Faith, including the scientists he worked with. Secondly, he could ask his superior at work for Fridays off for the remainder of the Five Year Plan so that he could pursue his travel teaching effort.

He had no trouble getting the day off. In fact, he was told he could use the company telephone for his Bahá'í work. When he insisted that they reduce his weekly salary by twenty per cent, his superior was startled, because no one had ever done that before. The company had been willing to pay him his regular wage. (About a month later he received a promotion and an increase in salary that more than compensated for the money he lost when he had his working week shortened.)

The young man and his family purchased a big, brick, colonial house in one of the more elegant neighborhoods of the city, because his Assembly had expressed an interest in reaching the more affluent segment of society.

'It is Bahá'u'lláh's house', he said to some of his friends. The idea was to make it available to the Faith. He had extra thick wall-to-wall carpeting laid on most of the floor space so that if they ran out of beds their guests could sleep in bed rolls on a relatively comfortable surface. At times twenty or thirty people stayed over-night to attend institutes at their home.

But those institutes were held after a setback, which turned out to be a constructive lesson. A few months before moving into the new house, the young man attended a meeting for all propagation assistants. The Auxiliary Board member sensed that the normal gleam was missing from the young man's face. He didn't say anything, because anyone can have a bad day.

But it was more than a single bad day. He had been slipping spiritually for several weeks. He knew he was in trouble. One night he called the Auxiliary Board member about a problem related to his work as an assistant. The

Auxiliary Board member sensed a lack of sparkle in the young man, and asked, 'Something bothering you?'

'Not really', he replied.

'But you don't seem your old self.'

'Well, our teaching effort hasn't been going too well since we moved. No one seems to be coming to our firesides.'

'Are you deepening regularly?' the Auxiliary Board member asked.

'Sort of', the young man responded.

'What do you mean?'

'You see, I don't have time to deepen at home in the morning, so I lock myself up in my office at work and deepen there.'

'Why can't you do it at home?'

'Because our alarm clock is connected to our television set. Whenever it rings, the "Today Show" is turned on, and I find myself watching it.'

'Trying to deepen at work', the Auxiliary Board member said, 'is difficult, because your mind is geared to deal with work matters. Everywhere you turn in your office is a reminder of where you are. It's hard to concentrate on the Creative Word in such surroundings.'

'I see.'

'Try putting prayer and deepening ahead of everything else in the morning and see what happens.'

The young man heeded the advice. A few months later seekers started coming to firesides and a stream of enrollments soon followed.

Personal Transformation

Some of us feel that deepening works for people like the

young scientist but not for us. We want to do it, but resist doing it. It is something we don't mention to others, because the reason for our resistance is a personal matter. Often it has to do with our past. The so-called bad things we did plague us. To try to deepen, we feel, would be hypocritical. So we find ourselves in a tug-of-war situation. Guilt and unworthiness pull us in one direction and Bahá'u'lláh pulls us towards Him.

Actually, we deepen to become worthy. True, what was done in the past has helped to shape our attitudes and behavior – but they can change by delving into the Creative Word on a regular basis. But sometimes even an awareness of the power of the Creative Word to transform human beings doesn't move some of us to deepen regularly. We are prevented by a deep-rooted problem, stemming from a lifelong indoctrination that we are fundamentally evil. We grew up in a society that believed that human beings are born as sinners. As children, youths and adults we were exposed to that belief at school, church, at home, even at work. Through osmosis it seeped into our consciousness. The ones we loved and respected most demonstrated that belief. Intellectually we accept the Bahá'í principle that humans are potentially good. How refreshing, we think. But deep down we fear that we aren't able to accept the principle emotionally, that it is something perhaps our children will believe.

Nonsense! We can believe in the original goodness of the human being, too. To allow the poison of original sin to paralyze us spiritually is like being unjustly sentenced to prison for life. Through deepening, we can win our freedom.

The transformation that takes place through deepening and prayer requires steady effort. At first not much change is noticeable; and that may prove discouraging, especially for those of us who are impatient and secretly yearn for a carefully drawn blueprint that produces immediate positive results. Bahá'u'lláh provides the individual who deepens and prays with some idea of how change comes about: 'Though he may, at first, remain unaware of its effect, yet the virtue of the grace vouchsafed unto him must needs sooner or later exercise its influence upon his soul.'[26]

Obviously most of us want to change for the better, to rid ourselves of character flaws developed before taking our Faith seriously. Some of us, who have tried to will them away and failed, are reluctant to try again, because failure can undermine confidence and cause long-lasting pain. But applying a divine remedy is far more powerful than resorting to human will. Without heavenly support, we end up psychologically flagellating ourselves; and to avoid feeling sorry for ourselves we adopt a superior attitude to others, become self-righteous and critical of those who aren't achieving what we are in terms of character development. To be good becomes an emotional strain. With some, the strain is so intense that they break down, ending their program of personal development and reverting to some of the character flaws they tried to eliminate.

For a Bahá'í, personal transformation operates differently. It is like being involved in a process where growth and shedding take place simultaneously. As we grow in our understanding of the Creative Word, our flaws are shed.

For example, a young man is touched by the Message of Bahá'u'lláh and becomes a Bahá'í. But he's a liar. He has always lied, because his parents lied, as did their parents. Lying was a natural part of their lives, used as a tool to survive in a hostile society. So lying had been ingrained in the new Bahá'í. He couldn't be kept out of the Faith because of a character flaw, for if that were the case, then most of us would be barred from Bahá'í membership.

As a Bahá'í he discovers that 'truthfulness is the foundation of all human virtues'.[27] He vows to change. But how to do it?

Realizing that through deepening and prayer he can be 'endowed with a new eye, a new ear, a new heart, and a new mind',[28] he decides to deepen every day – in the morning and evening as Bahá'u'lláh prescribes. He reasons that he must follow what Bahá'u'lláh urges us to do, because He knows, better than anyone else, what would help him carry out his vow.

So he begins to deepen, making time in the morning before going to work, and making time in the evening before going to bed. He even buys an alarm clock, to make sure he gets up thirty minutes before his usual time. A week after he starts deepening, he's tested at work. His foreman asks a question, and he lies, the way he did in his pre-Bahá'í days, without hesitating an instant. But when the foreman leaves, he realizes that he lied, something he would never have concerned himself with in the past. His new awareness is not only a sign of progress in overcoming a character flaw, but also signifies the development of the young man's conscience.

A month later – still deepening every day – he's tested again. This time he hesitates before answering a co-worker, wondering if he should tell the truth or lie. He succumbs to the pull of the past and lies, and for a few minutes feels bad for not having the strength to beat back his natural inclination. Though he lied, the young man is making progress.

He continues to deepen regularly. Three weeks later, he's faced with another test. He lies again, but this time, before he utters a word, his chest and throat tighten and he can't look at the person. Afterwards he berates himself for more than an hour for not telling the truth. Obviously, more progress.

Three months go by. Still faithfully deepening, he's confronted by a former friend about a matter that took place before he was a Bahá'í. He wishes he could disappear. The friend senses his uneasiness and wonders if he's ill. In a way, he is ill, for the thought of lying makes him nauseous – but he lies. For the remainder of the day he's conscience-stricken, even has difficulty sleeping.

After a year of deepening, a process he has learned to enjoy and now wouldn't think of missing, he's tested again. This time he's seized with pain in his chest and begins to sweat. His hesitation is so long that the person he's talking to asks the question a second time. In torment, he sits down, placing his head in his hands. He wants desperately to tell the truth, yet feels the tug of the past.

Suddenly, he opens his eyes, looks at the foreman who is standing over him and tells the truth. The pain in his chest disappears. There's a glow in his eyes. He feels like dancing. The foreman is perplexed, wondering if the young man is on some kind of narcotic. He has never seen him so happy. It is a victory only the young man can appreciate, a feeling of liberation he has never experienced before. He is not what he was before he started deepening. He sees and hears things that he didn't see or hear before. How could he ever go back to what he was? Never! For he has sensed the fragrance of the Abhá Kingdom. But this new awareness didn't emerge instantly. It wasn't something that he obtained as one would purchase a coat to protect oneself from the cold. The potential to be what he is now was always a part of him. By deepening he simply nurtured and cultivated the seed of happiness that he was born with.

Part of his new understanding is a belief in the process of deepening. It would be foolish to abandon it, because doing that would be like ceasing to water a rose plant that has produced its first bud. To stop would be to commit spiritual suicide. He knows now that it is something he must do for the rest of his life; and the prospect of doing that forever excites him, because of the guidance he'll receive, the insights he'll get, the growth he'll experience. With the beginning of each day he'll await with eagerness the new adventure Bahá'u'lláh has in store for him. He will be a joyous being, sincerely interested in serving others, and deriving genuine pleasure from doing so. A growing desire to teach will replace his natural resistance to sharing the Message; and he'll look forward to every teaching opportunity. Because his yearning to teach will evolve into a state of mind, he will be assisted by the Concourse on High to attract seekers into the Cause of God. Often innocently, without conscious knowledge, an unplanned encounter with a stranger will lead to the flowering of a new believer.

Deepening and Effective Teaching

A Bahá'í in one of the most remote sections of Virginia has had such encounters. He, like most other residents in the area, uses wood to heat his home. Fortunately, timber is plentiful on his property, but the trees require pruning from time to time.

One day the Bahá'í was out in his yard with a borrowed chain saw, determined to cut off the huge limb of a massive oak tree which was precariously perched against another tree near his house. After sawing off the twigs, he took a few steps back to plot his next move. Suddenly, a tall young man appeared, surprising the Bahá'í because he lived on a lane where there were no other houses. As far as he could remember no one had ever walked down the road before, or since, for that matter.

The man seemed friendly, and the Bahá'í asked his advice. 'How do you suppose I can get this limb down without it crushing me?'

So there they were, standing with their arms folded, their caps pushed back, eyeing the oak with the immense, dangling limb. After a few moments, the young man said, 'My truck broke down, up the road a piece. If I can get her started we can pull that limb down with my chain.' That's all he said, and left.

Half an hour later, the man returned with his pick-up truck and chain, and they completed the task in short order. 'How kind of him', the Bahá'í thought. He thanked the man and asked him to return any time he wished. The man drove off.

At the time the Bahá'í wasn't aware of how deeply touched the young man was by meeting him; nor did he know that the man was undergoing the most trying period of his life, that he had been contemplating suicide.

As the young man drove down the country road, his heart quickened as he recalled what had just happened to him. 'There was something about that guy that's special', he thought. 'There was something about his eyes. I've got to meet him again.'

And he came back in his truck, to take his new friend and his pregnant wife on a tour of the backwoods where the dirt roads are really paths, bumpy paths.

He continued to visit them and gradually he unburdened his heart. One night he asked, 'Do you think I'm crazy?'

'No', the Bahá'í said, pausing for a moment, trying to find the words to help open the young man's spiritual eye. 'No, I think you're seeking.' And he proceeded to tell him the story of Mullá Ḥusayn and his search for the Promised One. Why he chose that story on that occasion he didn't know. Nevertheless, it touched the young man deeply, and he responded in his thick, rural Virginia accent, 'I felt a lot like Mullá Husayn meeting the Báb when I met you.' A few more visits and the young man was a Bahá'í.

But that's not the end of the story. Becoming a Bahá'í was not easy for him. Less than a week after he embraced Bahá'u'lláh it was New Year's Eve. Thinking that he could avoid the temptations of parties and friends, he decided to spend the evening at home. Little did he realize that a party was going to be held at his house, and that his sisters had gone out of their way to buy him his favorite brand of liquor.

To run out on his friends wouldn't be right. For several hours he stuffed himself with cake. But by ten-thirty p.m. he reached for the telephone and called the Bahá'í couple. When they invited him to their home, he slipped out of the party and drove to the house with the massive oak tree.

And what followed was an evening of prayer and thanksgiving that he had survived his first test as a Bahá'í.

His friends, of course, had thought it strange that he, usually the 'life of the party', was stone sober.

Divine Assistance

Reading about teaching successes following a believer's commitment to deepening is inspiring, but it could reinforce our feelings of inadequacy also, especially for those who find reading difficult. A woman from Ohio was plagued with that problem. After listening to a recorded talk by an American Auxiliary Board member she tackled the problem head on. In a letter to the person who had inspired her, she described how she was assisted in overcoming her difficulty:

> I was one of those nine-year-old Bahá'ís who didn't know what the Covenant really was. I realized that you were right. I must read the Writings every morning and every night! I must pray steadfastly every day! Several times a day! I cried a great deal that night.
>
> The next week, my husband and I answered the call from Joliet, Illinois for travel teachers. The first person I talked to became a Bahá'í right away. I thought it was so beautiful but in the back of my mind I kept thinking that I wasn't praying or reading the Writings enough.
>
> When I got home I tried to read the Writings every day, but I had a problem. My reading level was lower than that of a sixth grader [twelve-year-old]. To read, for me, was like watching a movie in slow motion. I would soon give up in frustration. But then I would play the tape again and this would renew my energy to try.
>
> One night, I was in bed trying to read the Writings and it was very slow. I dropped the book and cried. I raised my hands and cried out, 'God! Increase my astonishment! Allow me to read your words! If this is what I am meant to be doing then allow me to do it!' I was so sincere that the tears would not

stop. The spiritual feeling that came over me is indescribable. For some reason, I could not stop crying these tears of absolute joy.

The very next day *I could read*. I could read as fast as I wanted or as slow as I wanted. I could read aloud (something which I could never do before). I could read the Writings of Shoghi Effendi and comprehend them. It was so beautiful.

NINE

Everyone Can Teach

Living in a time when career specialization is emphasized, we are conditioned to think that everyone must pursue a specialty. Such thinking inhibits us from exploring other areas. We grow attached to the notion that there are things we are trained to do, and things we aren't equipped to do. Unfortunately, this attitude is reflected within the Bahá'í community. It's a process spawned from cultural custom and tradition, and prevailing secular thinking, which creates an operating procedure — not devised by any divinely ordained institution — that departmentalizes, to a great extent, our contributions to the Faith. Quite wrongly, we are known as administrative Bahá'ís, consolidation Bahá'ís, proclamation Bahá'ís, minority-teaching Bahá'ís, praying Bahá'ís and teaching Bahá'ís. In the minds of most of us, including members of our Assemblies, we fall into special categories. We do this because we are accustomed to doing things that way. Certainly no harm is meant, but unbeknownst to us the teaching effort is impeded.

First, because there is no basis for this categorization in the Writings. Secondly, the number of teachers is reduced.

Instead of relying on everyone to teach, only those with the reputation of being teachers are expected to teach.

Further, those who don't consider themselves teachers grow more and more convinced that they aren't teachers when they don't teach. There is truth to the adage that 'practice makes perfect'. What is more worrisome is the fact that all divine assistance is cut off from those who don't share the Message. Without assistance, we are bound to have serious community problems.

In earlier chapters, we mentioned the importance of developing a Bahá'í attitude that dominates the way we live. With such an attitude, we won't succumb to popular trends that are counter to the aims of the Faith; and we won't allow ourselves to become categorized as non-teachers.

Often this categorization is self-induced, stemming from a lack of confidence, a fear of failure, a fear of rejection, a feeling that, somehow, we don't reflect the accepted image of a teacher. And we are afraid of making mistakes or a poor impression upon a seeker. So we look for the so-called 'best teacher' to do the teaching.

Who is a best teacher? The Guardian, in a letter written on his behalf, answers that question: 'A "best teacher" and an "exemplary believer" is ultimately neither more nor less than an *ordinary Bahá'í* who has consecrated himself to the work of the Faith, deepened his knowledge and understanding of its Teachings, placed his confidence in Bahá'u'lláh, and arisen to serve Him to the best of his ability.'[29] 'An ordinary Bahá'í!' That's us. We may read that statement, perhaps twice or more, and doubt whether it really pertains to us. 'Maybe to everyone else,' we think, 'but certainly not to me, because I know my weaknesses.' But the statement refers to all of us. There are ordinary Bahá'ís with less education than many of us, who don't earn very much money, who work in socially less desirable jobs, who attract people into the Faith. Their teaching exploits aren't publicized. They tell the Bahá'í story, in action and word, because they love God. And as that love grows through deepening and prayer, they become more and more effective in teaching. They are successful because they are recipients of divine assistance. And that assistance knows no age limits, as a Brooklyn nursery school teacher discovered. A boy of two, caramel-colored and bright-eyed, was brought to class one morning by his mother. He stood close to her, crying. He didn't want her to leave, because he didn't like being left in a strange place. When his mother left, the teacher embraced him and said that it was okay for him to cry, but only for an hour – a rule he had no trouble complying with.

The teacher sensed that there was something special about the youngster. On his first day he exhibited a wisdom beyond his years. When the children were told to recite grace before eating a snack, the little boy asked to say a prayer he knew. It was a Bahá'í prayer. The beauty of the words, and the way the child expressed them, moved the teacher and impressed many of the children. Soon after, the boy stood out again, this time during a name-writing exercise. The teacher's aide – a teenager – was writing the name of each student on the blackboard. When she came to the Bahá'í youngster, he insisted that she write the name Báb, which he explained meant 'the Gate' in Persian. He even corrected the aide's spelling when she naturally felt that name should be spelled with an 'o' and not an 'a'.

When the mother arrived to pick up her son, the

teacher asked her to explain more about the Báb. She did – and invited her to her family's fireside.

It didn't take long for the teacher to become a Bahá'í. To this day, she's eternally grateful to her spiritual 'father' who, through the years, has remained close to her.

There must be many Bahá'ís in the world, young and old, poor and rich, unknown by the great majority of believers, who go about their tasks without fanfare, living a simple life, but who, because of their purity of heart and devotion to the Faith, are the source of spiritual attraction.

A university-educated Bahá'í met such a believer, an unmarried woman in her late fifties, who earned her livelihood as a maid. He knew of her for a number of years before recognizing her reality. This happened through an experience that helped him to understand himself better and to gain a profound insight into how teaching is executed.

The experience began to unfold at Green Acre. The man was speaking to a close friend, whom he hadn't seen for a year. Meanwhile, a woman rode up to the men on her bicycle and waited for the conversation to end. The fellow from New Jersey resented her standing near him; he preferred being alone with his friend. In fact, he felt she was being obnoxious, a feeling he knew other Bahá'ís shared. Actually, she hadn't broken into the conversation; she simply waited patiently, holding onto the handle bars of her bicycle. But the man she wanted to talk to wasn't so patient. To get rid of her, he turned to her and asked, 'Can I help you?'

'Would you be willing to speak at one of our meetings on Friday nights when you return to New Jersey?' she asked, turning to a page in her notebook and poised to write down the date.

He wanted to say that he wasn't available any time. But he couldn't, because he remembered a vow he had made before going to Green Acre. Because of a hectic work schedule during the year, he hadn't been able to teach as much as he felt he should have. Conscience-stricken, he had sworn that he wouldn't turn down an invitation to speak for the Faith in the New York City-New Jersey area. And the woman's community was in a fairly large industrial city in New Jersey. Though he said he would speak, he gave her a date in late November, hoping that she and her community would forget about the agreement. A lot could happen in three-and-a-half months.

But nothing happened to cancel the meeting. In fact, he had been mailed directions to the place. Several hours before he was to leave for the speaking engagement, he was wallowing in self-pity. 'What a waste of time and energy. No one is going to show up at the meeting', he thought. Besides, a good pro basketball game was on television that evening and he wanted to stay home to watch it. 'If only I had an excuse to back out of my commitment', he thought. It was a clear and balmy day for November. He had been hoping for a snowstorm. No viruses had invaded his body; he didn't even have a sniffle. And the car was functioning well. Reluctantly, he got into it after supper and drove the forty miles.

As he snaked his way through the grimy, old city in the dark, he found himself in one of the most run-down neighborhoods. A fear of being mugged seized him, as he parked his car about a block from where the meeting was to be held. Finding the apartment in the tenement building wasn't easy. It couldn't be found via the front entrance; a door on the alleyway side of the building was the only way to reach the apartment. As he stepped into the alleyway, he heard cats hissing and snarling. The beasts were competing for scraps of food in the garbage cans.

'Now, what am I getting myself into?' he wondered as he opened the door.

The Bahá'í woman greeted him with warmth and love, standing there at the entrance of the apartment, beaming in her neatly pressed dress. The apartment was ablaze with light. As he walked to the brown wooden chair where he was to sit, he marveled at how clean the place was. Though the oilcloth on the floor was frayed in spots, it was immaculate. The furniture was worn, but neat. On the table was a large plastic bowl with a cherry-flavored soft drink and two plates with salted crackers topped with egg and tuna salad.

He sat down and watched the woman pouring him a drink. The feelings he had harbored about her in the past were a distortion of her reality. What he was witnessing was a devoted soul in action. As she handed him the drink, he noticed the time on his wrist watch. 'If I stay another fifteen minutes and no one else shows up,' he thought, 'I'll be able to excuse myself, race back home and see the second half of the basketball game.'

He never got to see any portion of the game. People started to arrive, about ten of them, most of them seekers, representing different races, different economic and educational levels. He was amazed at the way they greeted her, with such love and respect. They obviously saw in her what he had been veiled from seeing. But the veil was being lifted, and his heart was pounding. He wanted to reach out and embrace this noble woman, because she had opened his eyes and had demonstrated to him what a true teacher was. It had nothing to do with academic degrees, professional experience and charisma. No thoughts of time, of the basketball game, of being mugged came to mind. He was enveloped by a light of love. Fighting back tears was a struggle. If he had been alone, he would have broken down. But he had to keep his composure for he was the guest speaker, the one who was going to teach that evening. But he knew who the real teacher was in that room, and he felt the others did, also.

About a month later he was at the New York Bahá'í Center and was introduced to a charming gentleman and his son. When he discovered that they were from the same city where that noble woman lived, he asked if they knew her.

The man smiled and said that he not only knew her, but that she was the one who had taught him and his family the Faith.

Fascinated by the small, humble woman, who had probably never given a formal Bahá'í talk, he tried to find out more about her. He learned that she had been an orphan as a child, didn't have much education, and had worked most of her life as a maid. And when she had finally secured what could have been a lifetime job with a wealthy Manhattan family, she moved to New Jersey, to a city where there was little need for maids. This 'ordinary Bahá'í' had crossed the river to New Jersey because the Guardian had made an appeal for home front pioneers during the Ten Year Crusade.

TEN

The Example of Great Bahá'í Teachers

There are times when we become annoyed with ourselves because we don't live up to our own expectations of a Bahá'í teacher. For some of us the pain is a lot more acute, because we feel like failures. Teaching paralysis seizes us, a self-induced malady. We refuse to teach, because we don't want to fail again or to represent the Faith poorly. So we stand on the sidelines of the teaching arena, watching, hoping and praying and looking forward to reading about the teaching victories around the world in Bahá'í publications. 'At least some Bahá'ís', we think, 'are meeting success.' And we mentally cheer on those valiant believers in other places. But those we admire are not much different from us, and there's a strong possibility that at one time they were also seized by teaching paralysis. It is safe to say that many Bahá'ís have entered, left and re-entered the teaching arena numerous times. Discouragement, lack of confidence, worldly distractions, self-dissatisfaction, may have been some of the reasons for leaving. But when we leave we carry with us wherever we go the knowledge of the importance of teaching. In a sense, we are haunted by that awareness; and it is a good thing we are, because there will come a time when that awareness will be intensified by something we read, or by something someone says – and we'll re-enter the teaching arena, not knowing how long we'll remain.

'If only we could develop that teaching consistency', we say to ourselves, because fluctuating in and out of the arena is painful. We read and hear about the great Bahá'í teachers, people like Louis Gregory, Hooper Harris, the Kinneys, Lua Getsinger, Martha Root, May Maxwell, Roy Wilhelm – and we want to do the heroic things they did for the Faith. But we castigate ourselves for falling short instead of taking the time to find out what made those teachers so outstanding. They certainly didn't look alike, and their personalities were different, as were their social and religious backgrounds. And some were poor; others had wealth. They were as different from each other as all the believers are today. But they had one thing in common: they tried as hard as they could to follow the example of the perfect teacher, 'Abdu'l-Bahá. They heeded the Master's appeal to all the believers: 'Look at Me, follow Me, be as I am.'[30]

They knew they could never be the 'Center of the Covenant' or the 'Mystery of God'. And they also knew that to be like the Master didn't mean they should wear the same kind of clothes, eat the same kind of food, walk, talk or gesture like Him. To be like 'Abdu'l-Bahá, they felt, meant to do as He did in order to live in the world of the spirit – and that was to work continually at perfecting the divine attributes within themselves, a process wholly dependent on understanding and putting into practice the standards revealed by Bahá'u'lláh. So they prayed and deepened daily, as the Master did, and they grew firmer in the Faith, more fearless in dealing with the world, more sensitive and wise in interacting with people, drawing closer and closer to God, relying on His guidance in directing the affairs of their lives. They taught, as the Master did, because teaching was a commandment of Bahá'u'lláh's. To them, the fact that through teaching the human family would be united was of secondary importance. Obedience was their watchword; applying the Revelation to their lives was their primary goal. As they did this, their desire to teach grew until it consumed them, not as fanatics, but as spiritual physicians, their enthusiasm and knowledge drawn from the Abhá Kingdom. What else could have made the frail Martha Root cross the mighty Andes mountains in winter, on a mule, or remain in Shanghai, China, as Japanese bombers pulverized that city – all in order to fulfill her commitment as a Bahá'í teacher?

'How do I do it?' she once wrote a friend.

Every breath, almost, is a prayer to be a channel so that Bahá'u'lláh can do His work. The secret is, be ready when your opportunity comes.

If I do not read the Holy Writings, if I do not pray much, in two or three days I see the difference, the work is not so good. 'Work done in the spirit of service is worship,' I know, but the spirit must be nourished constantly. Sometimes I fail, but I KNOW the way to interest people in the Bahá'í Teachings is through love and deeds rather than through too much information . . . They themselves will ask fully when they are really attracted . . .[31]

ELEVEN

Personal Teaching

As Bahá'ís we have the responsibility to teach. We know
that. It need not be something dramatic. In fact, for most
of us it is a rather mundane endeavor; and we wonder
why we can't travel to every continent to share the
Message with secular and religious leaders as 'Abdu'l-
Bahá and Martha Root did. Most of us can't, because we
simply are not in the position to do it. Certainly God
knows our situation.

What is most important is to develop a consciousness
of teaching and do it wherever we live and work. It can be
just as meritorious to teach successfully in one's neighborhood or town as it would be to teach on a global level. For
so much is involved. Motive is one factor; and the practical ability and freedom to leave one's town is another.
Obviously, abandoning one's family isn't wise.

Teaching under Difficult Circumstances

Mobility isn't always needed to carry out the teaching
process. Even a physically handicapped person, one who
is bedridden, can be an effective teacher. There are

always nurses, physicians and relatives to teach, if not by word, then by deed and attitude. The paraplegic Bahá'í who wakes up in the morning with a yearning to share the Message of Bahá'u'lláh with someone – although there's no one immediately to share it with – is teaching; for what matters is that he is conscious of the need to teach and yearns to do it.

With such an attitude, God provides the opportunity to share the Message. An errand boy may appear, or perhaps a mailman, a long-lost cousin or neighbor. Or God may find another way.

Jost Stieldorf of West Germany taught the Faith from his hospital bed. A fellow Bahá'í witnessed it:

It is not often that one is present when an angel is born into the next world. The lovely youth had leukemia. While the cancer was slowly draining his strength, he grew calmer and stronger. His wonderful laughter was catching and spilled with such profusion that it seemed like a marvelous crystal brook . . . When the pain grew worse, he wrote to friends and family – always loving and consoling, asking them to drink of the cup of belief. . . For the Bahá'ís it was painful. Those who had heard him pray before were always amazed at the earnestness and fervor of his plea for mankind to be united . . . While in the hospital, though the pain must have been burning within him, he never lamented . . . He smiled at each [one] as if to say, 'I love you very much.' He emanated such love and warmth that it was hard to leave him in those last hours . . . It was during a prayer that he took his last breath . . .[32]

How can anyone deny that Jost Stieldorf was a Bahá'í teacher, or the scores of believers who heeded the Guardian's appeal to pioneer to a land where mentioning the Faith could lead to imprisonment or deportation, maybe death.

In such a country the authorities knew who the Bahá'ís were, and they watched them for twenty-five years. Because they found the Bahá'ís trustworthy and honest, dependable workers, people who contributed creatively and constructively to the country, many restrictions on the Faith were lifted. In fact, government officials were so impressed with the Bahá'ís that they sent their children to a Bahá'í school in a different land, on the grounds that there they would receive proper moral training. Native people also embraced Bahá'u'lláh. The Bahá'ís, who at one time couldn't utter the word Bahá'í, in reality always taught there, by example. While loving and serving the people they came in contact with, their hearts swelled with the desire to share the Message – no doubt a wish transformed into a prayer that was answered.

Each One Can Teach One

Fortunately, most of us live in lands where we can teach the Faith openly. Consequently, it is much easier for us to heed 'Abdu'l-Bahá's appeal to guide one soul into the Cause a year.[33] He doesn't ask that we attract more than that.

'If every Bahá'í took to heart the Master's appeal,' a member of the International Teaching Centre told a gathering of the United States National Spiritual Assembly and Auxiliary Board members, 'there would be no need for teaching plans. The number of Bahá'ís would double annually.'

One believer, an engineer, computed that if every Bahá'í complied with 'Abdu'l-Bahá's exhortation, everyone on our planet would be a Bahá'í in eleven years.

Obviously, it doesn't take an abundance of resources

to teach one person a year. We all have the means to do it, even if we think we don't. The confidence and will to do it come when we pray and deepen regularly; and then, despite our shortcomings, we eventually will go forth gladly, sharing the Message radiantly, happily, as one would give a gift to a lover. This is what a pioneer to Paraguay does day after day. She no longer thinks about the importance of teaching; she does it, because it is like breathing.

Considering that she was abandoned by her husband in the United States, broke her hip in Bolivia, was robbed and severely beaten in Columbia and has cancer, she has good reason to complain, but never does. Rather she's the willing ear to others who have problems. Those who know her have never heard her say an unkind word about another person. If someone attempts to backbite, she gently changes the subject. Though in her late seventies, she is an inspiration and example for all who are fortunate to be in her presence. And she longs for people – anyone – to come to her because she can't walk well. The beating in Columbia left her knees permanently damaged, and five operations on her hip have taken their toll.

When the house she was living in was sold, the friends insisted that she move to the Bahá'í center in the capital city. It is there that she executes her simple teaching plan daily. After awakening, she recites this prayer revealed by 'Abdu'l-Bahá: 'O Lord! Open Thou the door, provide the means, prepare the way, make safe the path, that we may be guided to those souls whose hearts are prepared for Thy Cause and that they may be guided to us. Verily, Thou art the Merciful, the Most Bountiful, the All-Powerful.'[34]

Then she unlocks the front door of the center – and

waits. Usually people she has never met before come through the door, and she teaches them the Faith. A young American friend watched the elderly woman guide a university student and a middle-aged man into the embrace of Bahá'u'lláh. And the woman was even ready for two German-speaking Swiss airline hostesses, giving them pamphlets in their language. After a while, the young American friend learned what made this woman such a powerful magnet. First, she continually sought Bahá'u'lláh's help. Second, she not only studied the Writings regularly, but she took to heart the Guardian's guidance on deepening: 'To deepen in the Cause means to read the writings of Bahá'u'lláh and the Master so thoroughly as to be able to give it to others in its pure form.'[35] And she followed the advice of an old friend, Curtis Kelsey: 'All you have to do is love.'

True, not everyone in our present spiritual condition can do that, but potentially we could. We can do a lot more than we think we are capable of doing. A way to emerge from the non-teaching doldrums is to make a serious attempt to heed 'Abdu'l-Bahá's plea to teach one soul a year. But many of us hesitate, wondering, 'Where do I start? What do I do?' We may also be plagued by the fear of forcing ourselves upon our friends, or the fear of being viewed as religious fanatics; and we may be shy, or doubt our capacity to teach anyone.

By growing closer to the Sacred Writings, we can progress in overcoming our reservations, shyness, doubts and fears; and the desire to teach will become a stronger feeling than our shyness and fear. Even if we don't know all the Faith's laws, we can still become effective teachers – if we sincerely love Bahá'u'lláh and are faithfully deepening in the little we know.

That's what happened to a Texan who was a hard drinker and a mean saloon scrapper. When the young woman he was living with took him to a fireside in Houston, he was so touched by the story of Bahá'u'lláh that he became a Bahá'í that night. He left Houston with a general knowledge of progressive revelation, some historical facts, a prayer book and an understanding that every Bahá'í has an obligation to teach.

He didn't waste any time before starting a fireside in the efficiency apartment he shared with his lady friend, who was pregnant with his child but married to someone else. Twenty to thirty people, many of them tenants in the apartment complex, flocked to the fireside.

In six months, ten people declared. News of what this new Bahá'í was doing spread throughout the city. The Unitarian Church asked him to speak about the Faith to its congregation. Though he hadn't finished high school and was an unskilled laborer, he addressed the well-educated group at the church. Had he not believed in Bahá'u'lláh, he would have never taken on such a challenge. Since no one became a Bahá'í on the spot, he felt his talk had been poorly received. But one man was impressed enough to attend his fireside regularly for six months. Though he didn't become a Bahá'í during that time, a number of his friends did.

While generating all this successful teaching activity, the young man didn't stop visiting the tavern and drinking with the 'boys'. He continued to take heroin from time to time, and the woman he was living with, who was also a Bahá'í, was growing bigger with child. The trouble was that he didn't know he was breaking Bahá'í laws, because no one had told him about the laws. But he prayed, and he prayed with all his heart and soul.

In fact, he said all three obligatory prayers every day, because no one had told him that he had a choice of which one to say.

When he learned about the laws and the administrative order, he immediately stopped drinking and taking drugs; and he and his lady friend wrote to the National Spiritual Assembly, seeking guidance on what they should do about their relationship in the light of their obligations as Bahá'ís. They were ready to live apart.

The National Spiritual Assembly responded in a compassionate manner; an annulment of the woman's marriage proved to be possible and she and her former hard-drinking, tough-talking, hot-tempered boy friend had a Bahá'í wedding. Three days later their first child was born.

As this couple continued to deepen and pray, their firmness in the Covenant grew, and their lifestyle changed. He went to college to study management. Not long after graduation, they moved to a different city, where he now owns a successful business and serves on the Local Spiritual Assembly.

Obviously, most of us won't experience such a wild episode in our lifetime. But we can learn from the experiences of others, even those who do things we wouldn't do. When that fast-living Texan fell in love with Bahá'u'lláh, he immediately put into practice what little he knew. And he experienced success in teaching, despite his ignorance of the laws.

If we applied that principle in trying to attract at least one person to the Faith in a year's time, we might also meet success, although perhaps not in such a flashy manner as the Texan did.

Guidelines for Effective Personal Teaching

There are many approaches to effective personal teaching – as many as there are Bahá'ís, because we all have different characteristics and consequently express ourselves differently. What works for one person may not work for someone else. There is no special formula that can guarantee that the person we teach will become a Bahá'í. That blessed event is really a mystery that only God controls. Yet there are guidelines that could help those of us who are frightened by the responsibility of teaching, or who feel inadequate to teach. The guidelines are like a lamp in the darkness.

By applying the following guidelines, many of us may be able to fulfill our personal goal of attracting one soul into the Cause each year.

1. Pray and deepen every morning and evening.
2. Select a person to teach.
3. Once the selection is made, pray for the seeker every day.
4. Love the person.
5. Serve the person.
6. Be a friend to the person.
7. Be a 'balm' to his suffering.[36]
8. Have a Local Spiritual Assembly pray for the person.
9. Be patient.

The guidelines work for those who really try to follow them. That doesn't mean that everything will work smoothly; that during the process there won't be moments of doubt about whether we selected the right person, or about our ability to achieve the goal. There were those moments for a Massachusetts Bahá'í, but he persisted, because deep down he knew that 'Abdu'l-Bahá couldn't be wrong.

He chose a university professor who was married to a Bahá'í. He knew the man's wife was already teaching him as were many other people as well. But that didn't deter the Bahá'í from making the choice, because his choice resulted from prayer. How did he come to consider the professor? He had met him at a Bahá'í gathering and had been struck by the man's heartfelt concern for the world's worsening condition. It was obvious the man was seeking solutions but wasn't finding them. He had little respect for organized religion, and seemed convinced the churches didn't have the answers. An activist, he was channeling much energy into various causes for social reform, and doing it despite the lack of meaningful results. He had to do what he was doing, because it was better than doing nothing. There had been some worthwhile endeavors, like the time he had helped to establish one of the first Black Studies departments in a major American university.

The professor's deep spiritual capacity was noticed at a Naw-Rúz party. He showed up late, after the dinner, perhaps to make a polite call on some of his wife's friends. He stayed longer than he had planned because of what was unfolding before him. With tears in his eyes he watched the Bahá'ís – blacks, Hispanics, whites, Persians, old, young, even pre-schoolers – dancing and laughing without any pretence. The wholesomeness and racial harmony moved the professor to say, 'This is real.' The words passed from his lips as if he had discovered something he had been looking for for a long time, maybe a lifetime, and had given up hope of ever finding.

At that point the Bahá'í felt that the greatest favor he could do for the genuinely good-hearted professor was to help guide him into the Faith. So he began praying for him.

During his morning prayers and deepening, he besought Bahá'u'lláh to open the professor's inner eye and heart so that he could see and feel the Message; and he also prayed that the seeker gain the courage to truly investigate the Faith. The Bahá'í never missed a day praying for the professor. No matter where he was – in Montreal, Maine, South Carolina, in Chicago, on vacation. And there were times during the day – while walking, or at work – when he would think about the professor.

Although prayer was essential, the Bahá'í knew that he had to become the seeker's friend – a genuine friend – never adopting a recruiter's attitude, and never losing sight of the objective, which was to help the professor find happiness and the means to truly change the world into a united and peaceful planet.

In developing the friendship, he guarded against becoming patronizing or acting superior in any way. There was so much the professor knew that he was ignorant of; and the Bahá'í sought advice from him.

If two weeks passed without hearing from the professor, the Bahá'í would call him, to see how he and his family were. In time, the professor began sharing his concerns with the Bahá'í. His eldest son was having problems, and the professor wanted to know more about the Bahá'í approach to family life. When the son needed guidance on how to develop a career in television and films, the Bahá'í, a professional in those fields, volunteered to confer with him. His assistance to the young man was motivated by a sincere desire to help the youth, not as a means of drawing the father closer to the Faith. The youth was reaching out for help and the Bahá'í responded.

Concerned about the public schools' dwindling effectiveness in educating children, the professor organized a group of parents and, with their help, started a school. The Bahá'í offered moral support, supplied advice on publicity and inspired another Bahá'í to write a newspaper article about the unique school – which was published.

Though the professor's department chairman recommended him for a permanent position the Provost turned him down because of campus politics. That was a severe blow. After seven years of dedicated service to the university, his department and students, he had one year to find another position. He liked where he was living, and his wife had a job in the area. The house he had designed and was building was almost completed. When the Bahá'í heard of his friend's predicament, he called and suggested that they get together.

At a two-hour meeting, the Bahá'í suggested career routes to take. One was to apply to some of the prestigious liberal arts colleges in the area. The professor did. One of the places he approached, perhaps the best of the lot, hired him.

Changes in the professor's outlook toward the Faith became apparent, even to himself. At first he found Bahá'u'lláh's Writings difficult to comprehend. The language was too florid, too mystical. In time, however, he gained more appreciation of the Creative Word, especially the prayers. What really drew him closer to the Cause was the realization that prayer works. It was something he had never experienced before. Undoubtedly, his wife's steady example attracted him to her prayer book.

One night, worried about his eldest son, he prayed that the young man would find happiness. The next day the son, who had been out of touch for a while, called his father and said that he was happy and that he was gaining a better focus on life. There were other confirmations, and the professor marveled over a phenomenon he, as a scientist, couldn't measure or explain.

The Bahá'í kept inviting the professor to firesides, but never pressuring him. It wasn't a case of calling him every week. There were times when the seeker missed three or four firesides in a row. But the Bahá'í stayed in touch, and invariably the professor would ask who was speaking at the next fireside. If there was a topic the Bahá'í felt the professor would find interesting, he would make a special call.

The professor was an active participant at the fireside. His comments were provocative and his questions probing, but not in a disruptive sense. He was a true seeker.

Though he was impressed with the Bahá'í community, and said so openly, even at firesides, he had difficulty seeing how the small number of Bahá'ís could make any significant social and economic changes in the world. At one point, after an animated fireside, the Bahá'í was inspired to write a long letter to the professor, explaining how the Faith was changing things. The letter moved the professor.

It was obvious that he was struggling; for he was an intellectual, steeped in the humanistic tradition, a non-joiner, skeptical of utopian-type movements – though in his heart he knew that only a universally appealing philosophy could save humanity. From time to time, the Bahá'í and his wife (also a Bahá'í) would lend the professor books and articles dealing with topics in which he showed great interest.

Because of the professor's knowledge and genuine concern for the state of education, the Bahá'í invited the seeker to speak about education at his fireside. For the Bahá'í it was thrilling to see the professor begin his talk with quotations from 'Abdu'l-Bahá. A lot of progress had been made. But there was a time when he wondered if the professor would ever embrace the Faith. That was about a month after he began praying for him. Impatient, one night the Bahá'í scrutinized the professor's face to see if his praying was helping the seeker grow. He looked for a radiant countenance or a special gleam in the eyes. But he didn't find what he was looking for. Disappointed, the Bahá'í wondered if he had chosen the wrong person. In meditating about the situation, he snapped out of feeling sorry for himself when he realized that checking for signs of spiritual growth in another person was a form of judging him; and that it could make the seeker uncomfortable. Faith was required, much like a gardener who plants seeds. He waters them, feeds them, but doesn't dig them up to see if they are growing.

The Bahá'í realized that he wasn't going to make the professor a believer. That was all in God's hands. The Bahá'í's duty was to beseech God to help the chosen seeker to investigate the Faith openly, to serve him, to love him, and to be a real friend, to assist him in times of crisis – and to be patient.

When the professor signed his declaration card, the Bahá'í was consumed with joy. He realized that 'each one teach one' is not so much a 'one on one' experience, but rather putting ourselves in tune with the spiritual forces promised in the Writings which enjoin us to teach. Many people may choose the same person to teach, and while we may not consult with them or even know who they are, we are aware when someone accepts Bahá'u'lláh that we have been working in a mysterious, unified way with a host of other souls, and even with the Supreme Concourse, to help bring spiritual life to a soul.

There's no guarantee that following these steps will work for everyone who tries them. There will be cases where a year transpires and the one we have been teaching hasn't become a Bahá'í – and he moves away. It's possible he may meet the Bahá'ís where he has moved to and become a Bahá'í there; and we are unaware of what has taken place. Or perhaps the person never becomes a Bahá'í. So be it. At least we tried our best.

Of course, the 'each one teach one' process could take other forms. For example, a hardy soul, who has more free time than most of us, might select three people to teach; one at work, one at the bowling alley he frequents, and a next-door neighbor, providing all three with the same kind of attention. By the end of the year there's a greater chance he will have attracted at least one soul into the Cause, and possibly all three.

Some of us may resent that kind of approach, however, sensing that it smacks of reducing teaching to a game of percentages. There is the danger of that happening if the teacher pursues the end without regard to the means; if he is more concerned with body count than the enrichment of a soul. It doesn't matter how many people a Bahá'í tries to teach, as long as his motive is pure and he maintains a loving spirit and seeks divine assistance. If detached, he'll be more concerned with the seeker's feelings than his own and will truly serve the person's needs. And that could come in the form of introducing the person we are teaching to someone else, someone who is better qualified to reach the seeker. It is counter-productive to persist in teaching someone with whom we have nothing in common and who is bored with us. When we sense that happening, the sensitive teacher moves quickly to expose the seeker to another Bahá'í with similar interests and background. In a sense, it is like a gynaecologist referring a patient to a cardiologist. What matters most is that the proper treatment be given.

Being Audacious

Though the Guardian urges us to be audacious in teaching, most of us hesitate to take his appeal to heart. We fear becoming religious zealots, even though we know the Guardian's position on fanaticism. We are afraid of taking a chance.

But by audacious is meant being always ready to present the Message whenever an opportunity arises. Certainly our audacity is to be coupled with sensitivity and wisdom, for that's the way the Master taught.

Regular prayer and deepening can make even the naturally timid soul an audacious Bahá'í teacher. There is a middle-class Ohio mother of three children who is that type of person. A closeness to the Creative Word has produced in her a power that sometimes surprises her. In fact, after a teaching event, she'll often say to herself, 'I can't believe I said what I did.'

Perhaps her most dramatic experience took place on an airplane. She was headed for Chicago, an hour's flight. But getting to her destination that day took a lot longer.

Mechanical problems kept the plane on the ground an extra forty-five minutes. As it turned out, it was a good thing that the plane didn't take off as scheduled. Sitting next to her was a tall, well-built, smartly dressed man. 'Business executive, no doubt', she thought.

Waiting was annoying because it was warm inside the aircraft, and she was looking forward to the Bahá'í conference in which she was going to participate. But she soon forgot about her discomfort. The man next to her, who was reading a newspaper article about the US hostages in Iran, said angrily, 'All Iranians should be killed.' The man seated on the other side of him seemed to agree.

Though startled, the Bahá'í woman blurted out, 'Oh no!'

The man turned away from the newspaper and looked at her strangely, and asked, 'What do you mean?'

'You see, my husband is Iranian.'

The man didn't have to say he was sorry; his face showed it. But the Bahá'í woman had more to say. She knew he was embarrassed; and she knew he really didn't mean what he had said. It had been a genuine expression of anger and frustration about an injustice he found his country unable to rectify.

She told him that her husband was a Bahá'í, as she was, and that their fellow-religionists were being persecuted in Iran. And she gave him the Message. Halfway through the conversation he took out a pad and took notes. As they were approaching Chicago, she learned that he lived in Skokie, a Chicago suburb.

'If you want to know more about the Bahá'í Faith,' she said, 'you could contact my friend there.' She gave him the friend's address and phone number.

In a few days, the man contacted the Bahá'í in Skokie and was invited to her fireside. Several months later he declared.

When the Bahá'í woman from Ohio heard the good news she was elated, because she had had misgivings about the way she had shared the Message with the man. It was non-stop talking on her part through most of the trip. When they parted in Chicago, she felt that she had probably frightened him, and that he had listened only to make amends for his insensitive remark. It was a strange experience, because in talking about the Faith with him, she wasn't aware of monopolizing the conversation, and was oblivious of time. In fact, the plane ride seemed to take a minute, not an hour.

Based on the results, she didn't do anything wrong. Her reaction was healthy; certainly a lot better than feeling that she had triumphed. When we feel proud of our effort, the chances are the person we have taught has been overwhelmed, and he avoids the Faith. On the other hand, by being concerned about her teaching approach, the Ohio woman demonstrated sensitivity. Undoubtedly, the man was attracted to what she said, and perhaps even more by the way she said it. Her enthusiasm wasn't artificial; it wasn't a self-generated enthusiasm that some actors, salesmen and clergymen employ. At the time, she wasn't aware of her animated presentation, because she had plugged into the Abhá Kingdom as a channel for the Holy Spirit. And what flowed out of that channel unlocked the man's heart. How did she plug in? Most likely by sincerely seeking Bahá'u'lláh's help through the Greatest Name, or an appeal couched in her own words, or maybe it was a feeling directed to Him. And He responded, as He always does.

The Importance of Spiritual Preparation

Effective personal teaching hinges so much on prayer and deepening. A Bahá'í from America's southland, who has experienced teaching success, shared some beautiful insights on the subject with a close friend:

As I become more experienced in the teaching field, I am finding that teaching is essentially a very simple process. Bahá'u'lláh brings us teaching opportunities daily. He does all of the work preparing the blessed souls. Our only job is to have our eyes open when the opportunity arrives and seize it, because it may not come again. Our preparation is a spiritual one – daily prayer and deepening, because then we will begin to see with a 'new eye' and hear with a 'new ear'. We will learn to perceive beyond the surface words and appearances and respond to their [seekers'] deepest cravings. Then we need to listen deeply and help them to unburden their sorrow and longing, for I have yet to meet a prepared soul who has not suffered deeply. After that, all we need to do is to pour out our love, unadulterated love, and let time, our prayers and love for these souls do its work. In such an atmosphere of love and trust, the Message of Bahá'u'lláh can penetrate into the depths of a seeker's heart, because it is open. I remember just the other night I was becoming rather animated while telling a seeker (a new Bahá'í's former therapist) about Bahá'u'lláh. I stopped and apologized for being so enthusiastic. He insisted that I continue, saying: 'Don't hold yourself back – that is real – it is genuine.' As the Universal House of Justice tells us, people are so ready for this Message, 'knowingly and unknowingly'.

Finally, with all these souls who have become Bahá'ís recently, as well as our current seekers, one of the most important ingredients is a deep, personal friendship. One cannot escape that intimacy if one desires to truly teach the Cause. It is a commitment of love and time – but the rewards are terrific.[37]

TWELVE

Firesides

There's nothing more frustrating than starting a series of firesides where seekers rarely show up, or where if they do, they don't return. It's frustrating because we want to attract people to the Faith. We want to see it grow, because we know nothing else will help humanity undergo that organic change the Guardian said was needed before real world peace can be established. And the fireside is such an important teaching vehicle. But for many of us, the fireside doesn't produce the kind of results we expect. Maybe we expect too much, thinking that it should be the means of attracting hordes of people into the Faith. Others feel they have tried hard and have met with practically no success. So they give up holding firesides and try another method, or stop teaching altogether.

When most of us think of a fireside we automatically imagine a forum for teaching the Faith, never giving much thought to why the Guardian used the term fireside. Certainly he didn't expect the believers to have fireplaces in their homes.

Could it be that what the Guardian envisaged was a

Bahá'í household, regardless of material worth, creating the kind of atmosphere we experience sitting close to a burning fire? When that happens, we are usually overcome by a feeling of tranquility, a feeling of well-being; we are able, for a few precious hours, to free ourselves from the clutches of a hysterical world. Our minds are clearer, keener and more receptive to new ideas. Our hearts are less agitated.

The Guardian believed the fireside was the most effective means of teaching. Obviously, the challenge is to generate a warm, caring, loving atmosphere in our homes. Without it, we end up having a fireside in name only.

Creating the Right Atmosphere

In holding a fireside nothing is more important than creating the right atmosphere. After all, a fireside is supposed to be a haven where people who step out of the cold, cruel world feel loved, wholeheartedly accepted, really listened to; and whose feelings are acknowledged and thoughts respected. With that kind of atmosphere, people usually return, because they don't experience it elsewhere. And often they come back, despite having understood little of what was said at the fireside. Eventually the seeker realizes that there is a correlation between the ideas expressed and the spirit in the home.

There was always an attractive spirit at the home of Curtis and Harriet Kelsey, despite their lack of proper furnishings.

For years they were without a sofa in the living room, using wicker chairs instead, the kind of furniture you normally see in rustic summer cottages. But the lack of appropriate furniture didn't deter Curtis and Harriet from holding weekly firesides. In fact they never entertained any reservations about having Bahá'í meetings because of the house's simple and meager décor. The love and warmth that permeated that home made the interior of the house glow. Guests rarely remembered the primitive furnishings. It was the spirit that so impressed them that they would look forward to returning. Their closest neighbors, staunch Protestants, who were financially secure, and living in more substantial, richly furnished houses, were attracted to the Kelseys' odd-looking dwelling. Frank Fredericks, an arranger for the Paul Whiteman Orchestra and musical editor for Maestro Arturo Toscanini, and his wife Octavia were refreshed whenever they visited the drafty pink bungalow across the road from their large red-brick colonial home. They and their son Frank Jr. eventually became Bahá'ís. William and Margaret Brooks, who lived in the neighborhood near the Kelseys, in an English Tudor house, embraced Bahá'u'lláh. So did their three children, Margaret [Peggy], Bill and Jim. It wasn't only the spirit in the house that attracted the Brooks and Fredericks families: Curtis and Harriet prayed for their spiritual awakening, loved them and served them, especially in times of greatest need.[38]

That special spirit was generated wherever the Kelseys held firesides, during good and bad economic times, even later in their lives – in Florida – when they had all the proper furnishings. To them, holding a fireside was a necessary function of life. After all, the Guardian had urged the believers to hold one at least every nineteen days in their homes. For the Kelseys that kind of urging was viewed as a directive from God.

The atmosphere of a home is a reflection of the spiritual condition of the people who live there. Since the Kelseys' dependence on the Creative Word grew with every passing day, they reflected the Holy Spirit more and more. They would be the first to admit that the spirit in their home was due to the power of the Creative Word; and they tapped that power every day, as a desert dweller sips from an oasis stream. Prayer and deepening were a part of their daily schedule. They knew that without them the attractive fireside spirit would vanish.

The Effect of Firesides

Imagine what could happen to the world if the great majority of Bahá'ís held regular firesides and worked faithfully to create a spiritual atmosphere in their homes. Miracles would occur, the kind that a New Jersey carpenter experienced. Maybe to others his experience wouldn't be viewed as a miracle; but to him it definitely was, because he believes nothing else could have transformed his life so.

He was a heavy beer drinker, an avid hunter; a man who hadn't really mastered carpentry. He did the rough work, nothing that required sophisticated skill. Though he barely tolerated his wife's regular attendance at a weekly Friday fireside, he decided to go along one night. Evidently his beer-drinking pals were doing something else that evening.

The fireside was held in a comfortable home, nothing fancy. Big lavish homes made him feel insecure, for it reminded him of how inadequate he was, what a poor provider.

His preconceptions were immediately dashed, because he was made to feel completely at ease. He felt encompassed by a spirit of genuine welcome. He met a man about his age, with whom he seemed to have a lot in common: the man was also interested in mechanical things. A friendship developed, and the carpenter kept coming to the firesides because his new friend was the host.

About three months later, his wife startled him when she told him what his new friend did for a living. As long as he had worked in construction, he had never had a heart-to-heart talk with an architect, someone he secretly felt wouldn't take the time to talk to him.

His new friend was not only an architect, but an executive with a prominent international architectural firm. As long as he could remember, the carpenter had revered architects. To him they were unapproachable, people he never dreamed he could talk to, let alone befriend. The Bahá'í architect never flaunted his education; he listened to his friend with genuine interest. He saw the good in the carpenter and focused on it, disregarding his faults. He reached out with his heart in sharing the Message of Bahá'u'lláh.

The carpenter couldn't resist the outpouring of love from his new friend, and though at first he didn't particularly understand what was being said at the firesides, he made a concerted effort to listen. Soon he recognized that the Teachings were the cause of his friend's attitude towards him, his way of life, and the loving atmosphere in his home. It wasn't long before the carpenter and his wife became Bahá'ís.

When the atmosphere is right, the chances are the firesides will be held indefinitely. One New England couple held firesides for nineteen years in the same city, in the same home and on the same night. They were held even when the couple was on vacation. A trusted friend would be asked to act as host.

That fireside produced scores of Bahá'ís from all kinds

of people – political activists, middle-class housewives, college students and drug-users.

Though the host and hostess were highly educated – he was a psychiatrist and she a composer – people who could barely read and write and who teetered on the edge of civilization were attracted to the fireside and felt comfortable there. One young lady in particular tried to resist going to the fireside, but couldn't. Something she couldn't explain pulled her to the place. She had nothing in common with the people there, for she was into booze and drugs. 'They are talking all that strange spiritual stuff,' she would say to herself, 'but it feels good there.' Today she is a college instructor, serves on a Local Spiritual Assembly and is an assistant to an Auxiliary Board member.

People like that young woman knew that every Friday night there was a place they could go where the good in them was drawn out. It was a place where she truly felt at home, more so than in the apartment where she lived. Had that couple not held their firesides, she would have sunk deeper into the city's social sewers.

Hosting Firesides

One Bahá'í woman views her fireside as a festival for Bahá'u'lláh. On the day it's held, everything else is relegated to a secondary position. She cleans her apartment thoroughly, bakes cakes, purchases flowers; and enjoys every moment doing that, viewing the floor-scrubbing and furniture-polishing as an expression of love for Bahá'u'lláh.

On the night of her fireside, nothing else exists, in cluding television. In fact, she never even checks out the television schedule of the day of her fireside. It doesn't matter if a highly touted program is on. TV is simply out of her consciousness on that night. That wasn't the case for a young man who was inspired by her to hold firesides. When a program was on that he desperately wanted to watch, he would actually hope that no seekers would show up, so he could turn on the TV set. If a seeker did come by, he speeded up the discussion, or cut it short in order to see part of the program.

In time, however, the young man overcame this weakness by following what his mentor did in preparing for her firesides. Now he prays and deepens every day, and prays specifically for the success of his fireside. He never misses a day doing that. He also finds the time to invite people to the fireside by phone, always trying to make contact several days before the event.

The fireside program is planned ahead of time. He lines up the speakers at least two months in advance. It is done that way in order to give the speakers ample time to prepare their talks; also, by knowing who the speakers are going to be, and what they are going to speak on, the firesides can be properly publicized in the local newspapers and radio stations.

He makes sure the topics vary and are tied to the kinds of questions to which most people are seeking answers. The speakers are encouraged to talk no longer than twenty minutes, and to present the Message in such a way that seekers are stimulated to ask questions, or make comments. And the chairman plays a key role. He also makes sure that no one dominates the discussion, and tries to encourage everyone to become involved. Before introducing the speaker, he always gives a brief overview of the Faith's basic teachings for the benefit of newcomers.

Not all firesides are supposed to be alike. Many successful ones feature a speaker, while others have a discussion format; and some will alternate between the two, or use music to share the Message. Actually it really doesn't matter as long as the spiritual atmosphere is right. That's what a long-time Bahá'í discovered when he was a seeker attending three different firesides in Chicago.

Though no incense was burning at Ruth Moffett's fireside, it was the kind of place where one would expect it. Everything was low-key – the talks, the conversation, even the seekers' questions. There the mystical aspects of the Faith were emphasized. At Ellsworth Blackwell's fireside, the apartment was aglow, every light in the living room was on; there was lots of laughter, spirited discussion, embracing and shaking of hands. Social issues were stressed. The third fireside had a more intellectual tone, maybe because the host was a graduate student at the University of Chicago.

Though the three firesides were different, they were similar in terms of spiritual atmosphere. The seeker felt comfortable at each one. He was made to feel welcome, his views were respected, he sensed happiness and security, and was moved by the lack of strain between blacks and whites, Jews and Christians. Experiencing that helped him to deal with his own prejudices. But he gained more than that, something more crucial. All that love directed at him opened his heart, allowing God to enter. It was through those three firesides that he discovered his spiritual nature and how to develop it.

With some Bahá'ís, holding firesides has become a natural part of their lives. They simply have to have them. That's how a Californian couple who moved to New Hampshire felt. Starting a fireside was one of the first things they did when they arrived in New England.

It didn't take long before curious Yankees started attending the couple's firesides and enrolling in the Faith. That couple's success was an inspiration to the other believers in town, freeing them from a long teaching slump.

The couple's attitude helped to make their fireside successful. They believed it would be successful and took the steps to make it so. (Those steps have already been mentioned in this chapter.)

One distinguishing feature of the couple's fireside was the hostess's insistence, on the night of the fireside, on having every light in her house turned on, even in obscure hallways, places where visitors wouldn't normally venture. Her husband, an ex-banker, who had been conditioned not to be wasteful, acquiesced in his wife's demand. For how could he dispute what Vaffa Kinney had once told his wife: 'The Master told me – conserve on all things except light.'

We all know the old saying, 'Where there's a will, there's a way.' A New England woman in her seventies had the will and found the way. Shortly after her mother and husband died, she decided to pioneer to Bermuda. Though a costly place to live, she managed to remain on the island by fastidiously policing her financial resources as only a born and bred Yankee can. She didn't eat much and lived in a small apartment which contained a tiny kitchen, bathroom and bedroom. Having no living room created a dilemma, because she wanted to hold a regular fireside. It was something she had always done. In New Hampshire her big house had been an ideal place for meetings. In fact the friends in her community had used her home as an unofficial Bahá'í Center. When the term 'fireside' was mentioned, the believers automatically thought of her home.

What bothered the pioneer most was that she knew how the Guardian felt about fireside teaching, and she knew from personal experience that it works. But how could she hold a fireside in her apartment? 'Men in my bedroom?' she thought. 'Certainly not Bahá'í-like.' Something had to be done, because no one in the community was holding a fireside, and some of the friends had large living quarters. 'A pioneer', she thought, 'should set the example.'

She prayed. And the quick answer was clear: start the fireside. With some ingenuity, she managed to make the bedroom appear more like a parlor.

It didn't take long before the room was filled with seekers every fireside night. That was fine, but finding enough seating became a problem. She certainly didn't want to limit attendance.

A local believer sensed the problem and asked the pioneer if she minded switching the fireside to her home, a spacious dwelling. Of course she didn't mind. In fact, she was ecstatic, because another Bermudian was going to experience the joy of holding a fireside. 'And perhaps others', she thought, 'might be inspired to open up their homes for teaching as well.'

THIRTEEN

Travel Teaching

The Hoosick Falls Project

Not many people have heard of Hoosick Falls, New York. Yet to a small group of Bahá'ís that place had a profound effect on their understanding of travel teaching; to some, an everlasting effect.

One thing they learned is that travel teaching has nothing to do with how far you go, only whether you arise to do it. Working in the next town will suffice.

The group from the Amherst, Massachusetts area didn't go very far. They had been inspired by a Hand of the Cause of God to help some of the nearby states, like New York, to open new localities and form new groups.

They contacted the Eastern New York District Teaching Committee for a list of goal communities. Hoosick Falls was chosen because it was closest to Amherst, about seventy miles away, and the roads were fairly good.

A meeting of those who were interested in participating in the travel teaching effort was arranged. The area's Auxiliary Board member for propagation attended.

There was mature consultation. All agreed that lasting power was necessary, for they had been part of other teaching endeavors that fizzled after an enthusiastic organizational session. How to prevent that from happening? Enkindlement. That was the way. For they were aware of 'Abdu'l-Bahá's insight on the matter:

The teacher, when teaching, must be himself fully enkindled, so that his utterance, like unto a flame of fire, may exert influence and consume the veil of self and passion. He must also be utterly humble and lowly so that others may be edified, and be totally self-effaced and evanescent so that he may teach with the melody of the Concourse on high – otherwise his teaching will have no effect.[39]

They were aware that through daily prayer and deepening the flicker of the love of God in their hearts would eventually erupt into a fire and continue to roar. A commitment was made by all to pray and deepen regularly; and the vow was taken with the understanding that what they had agreed to do was an essential, practical step. It was the fuel that would make the engine run.

Sensitivity was also needed to assure a successful teaching effort. That meant that everyone involved should appreciate the spirit of the community and its people. Without such an understanding, damage, possibly serious damage, could result. It would be like someone trying to hit a target with his eyes closed.

How to gain the information required to develop a sensitivity for Hoosick Falls? None of the team members had ever been there, had even driven through the town. Someone volunteered to make a survey. He was an electrical engineer for a power company, who had several vacation days due him.

He rented a room at a local motel. Following the suggestions of the committee, he listened to the local radio station to gain a feel for the type of music the people preferred; he read the local weekly newspaper to secure a sense of the issues confronting the citizens. He ate at different restaurants, trying to engage people in conversation, without prying. He did some shopping in the local stores and checked out the different churches to determine what were the dominant religions. By stopping at the town hall, he was able to learn more about the number of people in Hoosick Falls, and something about its economic base.

At the next committee meeting, he revealed his findings, but he didn't share all of his feelings. He didn't, because he didn't want to discourage the friends. Deep down he felt that Hoosick Falls was a town that lacked vitality. In fact, it seemed to be decaying and was certainly provincial. No major highways were close by. Unemployment seemed high. The business section appeared deserted. There wasn't even a movie house. At one time it had been a thriving factory town, but the factories weren't operating any longer. 'It would take a miracle', he thought, 'for someone to become a Bahá'í in this place.'

Because one team member had been there, everyone else had some idea of what the town was like. But the committee felt that other people should make surveys as well, because from three or four perspectives a more accurate profile could be constructed.

The next two Saturdays two different survey teams visited Hoosick Falls, coming back with new information. For instance, one group discovered that the mayor was the local barber, a friendly fellow who volunteered lots of background on the town.

In a sense, his barbershop became the symbol of sacrifice for the male team members. Some of them had their hair cut there, thinking that perhaps that would help to create trust between the mayor and themselves. That kind of bond could be a form of protection for the Faith in the future. Amherst Bahá'ís who were not on the team could always tell who had recently been to Hoosick Falls, because of the way their hair had been cut. No sideburns. It was as if the barber had placed a bowl on their heads and shaved every bit of hair below the rim.

Continuity, the team members felt, was necessary if the project was to succeed. A visit had to be made to Hoosick Falls every week until a local person became a Bahá'í. To assure that a visit wasn't missed, a different team would go each week. It was a way of avoiding over-burdening a few souls who lived busy lives. No more than three or four people made the trip, because the committee didn't want the local people to feel that they had been invaded by some alien group. They also agreed not to mention the Faith unless it came up naturally. The idea was first to make friends.

The treks to Hoosick Falls started in early October. Before proceeding into the town proper, prayers were usually said at a cemetery on a hill above the community.

A full day was spent in the town, each team member going his separate way. One might go to the park and find someone to talk to. Another would spend time at the recreation center befriending youth. Someone else would visit different shops. One young lady had an unusual experience, though at the time it didn't seem extraordinary. She was at a bee farm, purchasing honey. It wasn't the bees or the honey that fascinated her. It was the handsome brick house on a hill overlooking the farm.

'Wouldn't that place make a wonderful Bahá'í center', she thought. She was destined to see that place again, but under different circumstances.

The committee received good news: the Amherst Local Spiritual Assembly had decided to help fund the Hoosick Falls project.

A month passed with nothing apparently significant developing. Some of the team members began to wonder to themselves if perhaps they had chosen the wrong place. Frustration was setting in with those who wanted to be more direct in teaching. But at a committee meeting, where feelings were openly expressed, everyone agreed that they needed to be more patient. After all they were doing what 'Abdu'l-Bahá had said should be done. 'Perhaps', one person said, 'we are being prepared to be used as channels; and there is still a lot of ourselves in the way.' Every team member continued to pray and deepen.

Early in November a team member noticed a poster advertising a panel discussion on violence that was to take place at a local church. He thought it would be good if other team members joined him at the event. 'Certainly', he thought, 'there will be people at the church who would be attracted to the Bahá'í Teachings.'

There definitely were, but the Bahá'ís weren't aware of them – at the time.

The panel attracted a large crowd, standing-room only. After the speeches, the audience was invited to share their feelings on the topic. A team member was recognized. After hearing the Bahá'í viewpoint on violence, without the Faith being mentioned, the audience was won over by the young man. They were so impressed that following the event leading members of the church thanked him for his contribution and urged him to return, because they found his views enlightening. Of course, what the cluster of admirers around the young Bahá'í didn't know was that they had been touched by the Teachings of Bahá'u'lláh. An important inroad had been made.

A few days later the young man was inspired to send the pastor of the church a letter commending him and his parishioners for holding the panel. This letter was posted on the church's main bulletin board for all to see.

Soon after, the committee met to plan the next phase; for the soil had been ploughed in Hoosick Falls and it was planting time.

Firesides were to start every other Saturday in nearby Bennington, Vermont. Why Bennington? Because Bahá'ís resided there, and a young woman had volunteered her home as the fireside site. Besides, most people in Hoosick Falls were accustomed to going to Bennington to attend cultural events.

News releases were given to the weekly Hoosick Falls newspaper – and were published.

A few weeks later a major breakthrough took place, involving the young man who had spoken at the church. He had wandered into a small gift shop that sold miniatures. The co-owner recognized him because she and her husband had attended the meeting on violence. It didn't take long before they were talking about the meaning of life and other weighty subjects. She was fascinated by his views and pressed him for sources. When he revealed that he was a Bahá'í, she appeared genuinely curious, much like a child given a gift in a pretty box, and wanting to know what was inside.

After hearing a brief description of the Faith, her enthusiasm grew, and she asked where she could learn more about the Faith. The young man gave her a pamphlet, wrote down the address and telephone number of the home where the fireside was going to be held – and invited her to it.

'Could I bring my husband along?' she inquired. 'And my business partner and her husband?'

Since the firesides weren't going to start for another three weeks, the young man made sure of keeping in contact with the shop owner, by telephone or by calling on her. Reading about the fireside in the local newspaper, she later told the Bahá'í, helped to reinforce her interest in attending the meeting.

On the day of the fireside, eight Bahá'ís went to Hoosick Falls: three college students, one youth, two middle-aged women and two middle-aged men, including the electrical engineer who had made the initial survey. Nothing could keep them from going, not even the committee's rule limiting the number of travel teachers. Incidentally, in the two-and-a-half months of the Hoosick Falls project, enthusiasm among the team members had increased instead of declining. Those university doctoral students who initially stated they could only commit one Saturday every six weeks were trying to go every week. They, like everyone else involved with the project, had become enkindled – due, of course, to regular prayers and deepening, and their wonderful experiences in Hoosick Falls which produced confirmations, one after the other.

One of the confirmations occurred about eight hours before the fireside. Two Bahá'ís accidentally met the gift shop owner in a pharmacy. Though surprised, she was obviously happy to see the Bahá'ís. When she said that her husband was helping the minister of her church remodel the children's Sunday School classroom, the Bahá'ís volunteered to help out, and went off with her.

The minister's reception of the Bahá'ís, who were introduced as such, was proper but cool. Evidently, the gift shop owner had been talking to the minister a great deal about the Faith. And it was obvious that the husband didn't share her enthusiasm for the Bahá'í Teachings.

Nevertheless, the young man and the Auxiliary Board member removed their jackets, rolled up their sleeves and began hauling wood and boxes to the basement. While working, the barrier that the husband had built around himself vanished, a fact that became apparent when he and the Auxiliary Board member started talking about their families and sports. The husband had been a college wrestler and two of the Bahá'í's sons had wrestled in high school. By the time they had finished working, the husband had warmed up to the Bahá'ís, and even offered to drive them to the florist where they wanted to purchase flowers for the hostess of the fireside.

As they were about to back out of the church's driveway, the minister appeared. He bent over the window on the driver's side and, staring at his highly-valued parishioners, said, 'I'm sorry you won't be at the church affair this evening.' He paused and with a note of sorrow and doubt in his voice, added, 'I guess I'll see you at the morning worship service.'

The fireside that night was a success. Six seekers showed up. Two from Hoosick Falls – the gift shop owner and her husband. She asked a number of questions, including, 'Can you become a Bahá'í and still retain your church membership?'

When the question was answered, she responded, 'I don't think I could ever become a Bahá'í, but maybe my children will.' Her husband didn't ask a question, but his face had the expression of a deep thinker. It was obvious that he was observing the people around him carefully, as well as the statements being made and the general atmosphere of the meeting place.

Just as the teams kept visiting Hoosick Falls week after week, the couple kept coming to firesides. Eventually, the husband began talking, asking probing questions; and the Bahá'ís began learning something about him. It turned out that he was a lawyer and an elder in his church, and that his wife also held a high lay position in the church. The couple were relatively happy with their religious affiliation. They certainly weren't involved in a desperate search for truth. But it became clear to the Bahá'ís and themselves that they had been moved by Bahá'u'lláh's Teachings – so moved that they eventually asked the Bahá'ís if they could celebrate the Ninth Day of Riḍván at their home.

It was an exciting affair. Some of their neighbors attended as well as a fairly large contingent of Bahá'ís from the Amherst area.

Soon the couple began holding firesides and teaching their three children Bahá'í prayers. That summer the couple enrolled in the Faith at the Green Acre summer school, and almost immediately started holding regular firesides.

A year and a half later they had attracted two local people to the Faith and another person from a neighboring town. Practically everyone in Hoosick Falls knew they were Bahá'ís and respected them for it. A leading nursing home in town asked the gift shop owner to conduct a course on spirituality for its residents; and her husband developed a popular study class on the Covenant for the Bahá'ís in the area, mostly isolated believers and members of small groups.

The last time the Auxiliary Board member who had worked on the project visited the couple, it was to speak at their fireside. As he approached the brick house on the hill, he recalled the wish that the young Bahá'í woman had had while at the bee farm two years before. Her wish had been fulfilled. That house was, indeed, the Bahá'í center she hoped it would be, because inside were more than thirty-five people, Bahá'ís and seekers, including seven members of the son's high school basketball team. It had become the place in Hoosick Falls that everyone identified with the Bahá'í Faith.

Travel Teaching in South Carolina

A northern couple and their teenage daughter decided to go travel teaching in South Carolina, a place where there are more Bahá'ís than in any other state in the United States. They were looking forward to making the trip, especially the husband who had heard that enrolling Bahá'ís there was as easy as picking fruit from a tree. He yearned for such an experience, because he lived in a community where two, maybe three, people enrolled in a year.

When the family arrived at the Louis Gregory Bahá'í Institute – their base of operations – they were greeted warmly by the director, and after being given a cool drink were handed a week-long itinerary. The husband tried hard to conceal his displeasure with the schedule, which called for more proclamation and consolidation work than teaching.

Their first stop was a familiar setting. It was an elegantly adorned home in a fashionable suburb of the state's largest city. The Bahá'ís they met, though black, white and Persian, were college-educated professionals. 'Where are the pure-hearted rural blacks?' the husband wondered.

After a forty-five-minute live radio interview, the family drove to a small city in the extreme southeastern corner of the state where heat and humidity dominated all life except for those who lived and worked in air-conditioned places.

The husband did a thirty-minute interview in an air-conditioned all-black radio station. It was also his first teaching opportunity; but it wasn't what he had antici-pated. The general manager of the station, a successful black businessman, was impressed with the Bahá'í teach-ings and approached the northern white visitor with several questions about the Faith.

'I believe what you say', he said. 'I have little respect for the churches here. There shouldn't be black churches and white churches here, or anywhere else. Everybody should belong to the same church. The Bahá'í Faith makes sense.' The man paused, and then asked, 'Do you have any books I could read?'

'We can arrange for the Bahá'ís in town to get you some,' the Bahá'í said, surprised at what was transpiring. He hadn't counted on sharing the Message with anyone in the media. He realized that Bahá'u'lláh had different plans for him, and from that moment on he stopped feeling sorry for himself. 'Let go!' a voice inside him said. 'Just let go!'

Before leaving the radio station, the northerner and his local Bahá'í escort were told by the general manager that he would like to give the Bahá'ís a half hour each Sunday morning to proclaim the Faith.

Outside the heat was oppressive. The northern family had every window completely open in their car, as they followed a local Bahá'í across a bridge leading to an island where a number of believers lived. The husband and wife had read about the place in the *Bahá'í News*. It had been the site of many teaching victories in the 1960s. As they twisted and turned on country roads, the South Carolina the husband had pictured back home came to life. So many signs of poverty. Small, unpainted, weathered houses, with sagging porches, dotted the landscape; most of them occupied by blacks. 'Some of them', he thought, 'might be Bahá'ís.'

The family's hostess that afternoon and evening lived in a white cottage with blue shutters. She was an eighty-six-year-old black woman who relied heavily on a cane to make it from one room to another. The arthritis in her knees was beyond surgical repair. But her physical disability hadn't affected her spirit. She embraced the Bahá'ís from the north as if she had known them all her life.

She hobbled ahead to the living room, with the northerners behind. Once in her chair, which was practically touching a rusting electric heater, she introduced her nine-year-old step-grandchild, who was seated in a chair reading a book. Though no 'blood relative', the girl was being reared by the woman.

'This child is the best student in her class', the old woman said. The guests soon discovered that the elderly woman wasn't exaggerating; and they also learned that the barefoot girl in a flowered beige sun dress possessed a wisdom far beyond her years, and a sweetness that sprang from a reservoir watered by a love of God. She recited Bahá'í prayers, read a few short Bible stories aloud and sang songs, some of which the guests had heard sung in Bahá'í children's classes back home. It wasn't a case of the child showing off, but rather an expression of happiness, a celebration of discovering new members of her family. And the three Bahá'ís from the north couldn't help but share in her joy. She was the breeze they had longed for on that hot day.

After that young luminous soul had showed the guests the old woman's family picture album, providing background on those she felt to be her uncles, aunts and cousins, she excused herself to fetch the bread pudding and lemonade her grandmother had prepared for the occasion. As she skipped into the kitchen, the old woman beamed with pride. Though they were not 'blood' relatives, they lived life as if they were grandmother and granddaughter.

It was truly a Bahá'í home. And everyone on the island knew it, because they knew how much the elderly woman loved Bahá'u'lláh. She had been a pillar of the biggest black church, a voice that everyone respected. Her acceptance of Bahá'u'lláh as the return of the Christ spirit had set off shock waves in the community. Others had followed her into the Faith.

Tacked to the wall above the entrance to her bedroom was a picture of 'Abdu'l-Bahá, facing a painting of Jesus Christ on the opposite wall. On a table next to her chair was a worn copy of *Bahá'u'lláh and the New Era*. After explaining how she became a Bahá'í, she closed her eyes and said, 'I thank the Lord for bringing Bahá'u'lláh into my life ten years ago.' Then she placed a hand on the book, and added, 'I'm willing this book to my oldest son.'

The supper she prepared for her fellow believers from the north was simple: a ham sandwich for the teenager, and a platter of cold fried fish with bones and head and tail intact – to be eaten by hand. It was something the guests had never tried before. 'Please take a fish', the woman said, moving the platter closer to the guests. The man ripped off a tail section; he couldn't eat the head, the part the woman favored. His wife followed suit. Both found the fish tasty, and the husband sucked the bones as his hostess did. For dessert there were large chunks of locally grown watermelon.

Two hours later the living room was packed with people, blacks and whites, including three seekers. The younger ones sat on the floor. Two fans whirred, trying valiantly to create relief from the hot, muggy air. But what really helped was the rain – sheets of it. After a few prayers, including one recited by the old woman, the group broke out in song – Bahá'í songs and old Negro spirituals. Everyone was stirred when the hostess closed her eyes and began a solo of 'Bahá'u'lláh is the Light of the World'. Love, admiration, devotion and awe emanated from that beautiful soul. All twenty-five people there, even those who didn't know the words, joined her the second time around. Clapping came naturally. Even the northern family couldn't resist that gesture of joy. Not even the thunder and lightning and the flickering electric lights could stop the singing. The teenage daughter, fighting a cold, was so moved by the spirit that she led everyone in several rounds of 'Amazing Grace'.

As her father was being introduced to say a few words

to the group, he abandoned his prepared talk on teaching. 'How can I tell these people what teaching is?' he thought. 'Just be guided by God.'

He talked about the relationship between Jesus and Bahá'u'lláh; and explained how he, of Jewish background, had grown to love Jesus through the Blessed Beauty.

The following day while driving to their next stop, where a television interview awaited them, the husband and wife came to the same conclusion: they weren't really on a teaching trip; their true mission in South Carolina was to learn about teaching.

Waiting at the site of the interview was a Bahá'í couple from a nearby town. From them, the northern family learned much.

The man's roots were in South Carolina, and he had never lived anywhere else. He had the kind of face that made you feel good inside, made you want to be with him; and it didn't matter whether words were exchanged. It seemed to the northern man that his host had taken to heart that appeal by 'Abdu'l-Bahá: 'Be happy and joyous because the bestowals of God are intended for you and the life of the Holy Spirit is breathing upon you.'[40]

The man was happy despite obvious evidence that he had endured considerable suffering. His left arm and left leg were partially paralyzed, the result of an automobile accident in 1975. But after being with him a while, you were no longer conscious of his handicap.

This interracial couple lived in a small town, in an area of the state where the Ku Klux Klan is entrenched and influential. The couple immediately enveloped their guests with whole-hearted love, showering them with kindness.

Because errands had to be done, the men went in one

car and the women in the other one. For the northerner it was an opportunity to be alone with this radiant soul who was behind the steering wheel. Eventually, the matter of the driver's accident was mentioned. 'In a way', the South Carolinian said, 'it was a bounty, because it forced me to quit my wayward habits and to rely on Bahá'u'lláh and do what he wants me to do.' To the man from the north, there was no doubt that the man next to him was putting the Faith first in his life. He could feel it.

Before reaching his town, the man started to point at houses along the road, saying, 'Bahá'ís live there', or 'Those are Bahá'í homes'; and then he turned to his Bahá'í brother from the north and added, 'There are three kinds of people living in our town – Bahá'ís, Jehovah's Witnesses and the Ku Klux Klaners.'

The women were already inside when the men arrived at the couple's house, a two-story red brick dwelling with two brick chimneys.

'We have ten acres and grow eatin' corn and butter beans', the host said.

But his guest wasn't interested in the crops. The remnants of a brick wall, about twenty feet in front of the house, caught the northerner's eye.

'That', the intuitive host said, 'was part of our first house.'

'What happened to the first one?'

'It was burned down just before we installed the electrical wiring.'

'Do you know what caused the fire?'

'No', the host said, smiling.

The northern family later learned from some of the local Bahá'ís that the Ku Klux Klan had been the arsonists, and that it had been done to discourage the interracial couple from living in town. When the couple started to rebuild, most of the blacks in town held special prayer vigils to prevent another KKK act of violence.

After a late lunch, a tall, slender white man, slightly stooped, wearing a baseball cap, came to the back door. He had been working in the fields all day under the torrid Carolina sun, and appeared flushed. The host urged him to come into the house. Before he sat down, the hostess was already making him a cold glass of orange juice.

With his hand on the white man's round shoulders, the host said to his guests, 'I'd like you to meet one of our local Bahá'ís.'

The northerner was stunned that a man like that would become a Bahá'í, because the farmer was to him a 'typical redneck', the kind of person who would burn crosses on a black's property. But he was even more startled when he learned that it was his host who had attracted the farmer into the Faith.

'How did you do it, you being black?' he inquired after the farmer returned to the fields.

'I just became his friend', the host said softly.

'What do you mean?'

'Well, we discussed things.'

'Like what?'

'Fishing, baseball, crops, whatever he wanted to discuss.'

'When did you mention the Faith?'

'Not for a while. It just came up naturally.'

The northerner thought of the appeals by 'Abdu'l-Bahá and the Guardian for the believers first to make friends and then share the Message. His host was patient. It was evident that teaching wasn't something he turned on or off, depending on his mood or the occasion.

Teaching was something he had integrated into his life and every waking moment was an opportunity to share the Message, if not by word then by deed, or by plainly 'being'.

But the northerner was to hear more about that white farmer and fellow Bahá'í. While driving into a nearby city to purchase medicine, his host told him that the farmer's brother and sister-in-law lived there, and that they were Bahá'ís also, having been taught by the farmer.

Telling someone how something is done is one thing; but observing how it's done is another, and a more effective means of learning. By joining his host at the local town semi-professional baseball game, an event that brings out most of the townspeople, the northern man witnessed how an effective teacher teaches.

Before the game started the host took his guest to a Bahá'í home to pick up the Vice-Chairman of the Local Spiritual Assembly, who was also a leader of the town's black community. While waiting for him to change clothes, the two men sat down under a large shade tree to talk with two men, one a Bahá'í, the other a fellow from a different town and not a Bahá'í.

The northerner tried to hide his uneasiness when the non-Bahá'í, wearing three diamond rings on his right hand, mentioned that he had spent time in jail and that another time he had had to win his freedom by paying off a judge after being caught with cocaine. But the host wasn't flustered. He listened to the man's problems, not only with his ear, but with his heart. He didn't make the man feel uncomfortable or inferior. The host proved that he could fit neatly into any situation without compromising Bahá'í laws. And because of his attitude, the man with the criminal record, who initially seemed hostile to the northern white man, grew affable and accepting of everyone there.

The Faith was mentioned only after the non-Bahá'í asked the northerner why he was in town. A brief explanation was given by the host, and the man became a seeker.

The Bahá'í from the north was the only white person at the baseball game. Both teams were black, and everyone in the grandstand was black. Between innings, the host introduced his Bahá'í brother to some of the spectators who dropped by to chat; and when he and his guest left, instead of taking the shorter way out, he purposely took the longer way – despite his crippled leg – so that everyone in the stands could see that the Bahá'ís believe in the oneness of mankind. It was his way of proclaiming the Faith.

There was more to learn from the interracial Bahá'í couple. After a hearty breakfast of grits, eggs and bacon, a white man appeared at the back screen door. He was heavy set, wearing a cap and the kind of clothes golfers wear on the course. He came by to pick up some fresh corn and butter beans grown by the host. It was a local custom to share some of one's crop yield to see who was producing the best tasting vegetables.

The man was invited into the house to join everyone for a cup of coffee. He was introduced by the host and hostess as a former neighbor of theirs from their previous home. The man and his wife would watch the interracial couple's house when they were overseas visiting her parents, or when they were on long teaching trips.

A pleasant conversation ensued. The host and hostess showed concern when they learned that the man's wife was recovering from surgery, but were relieved to learn that it was a minor operation. The man, however, seemed anxious about the move of his daughter and son-in-law to Philadelphia. Evidently, he had heard some frightening stories about life in the big northern cities. But the northern couple, who had lived in Philadelphia, explained what a wonderful place that city was and how much they had enjoyed it.

After the man left with the host to pick corn and beans, the hostess smiled and told her guests that the man was a member of the Ku Klux Klan.

The northerners were startled, for the man had been so gracious, so civilized. He had even taken off his cap before entering the couple's home.

'Amazing', the northerner thought. 'That guy genuinely liked this couple, yet he belongs to an organization that fights, often violently, to oppose black and white marriages. How can this be?' Then it dawned on him that it was the loving spirit of the couple that had won him over. And he realized that the couple had never uttered one negative word about the man, only mentioning the kind things he had done for them. To them, that man was a potential Bahá'í, and they treated him as such.

The northern couple would also never forget the impromptu children's class the hostess arranged in a town fifteen miles away.

A class was usually held at the weekends for the Bahá'í children and their friends, both black and white. But on this day no one was home. The parents were probably working that hot Thursday afternoon.

'The woman's mother – also a Bahá'í – must have the children', the hostess said, and drove a couple of miles to a secluded, heavily wooded lane and up a winding dirt road to a shack. The door was open. A gloom existed in that dark place that the northern man had never experienced before. An old black man, holding a twig, sitting on a mattress and shoeless, seemed lost in the intrigues of a television soap opera. A large black woman holding an infant was also mesmerized by the television. Neither adult was a Bahá'í. The children who were sitting on the worn wooden floor recognized the hostess and ran to her. Those who reached her first embraced her.

After learning that their grandmother was in the fields, the hostess received permission from the large woman to hold a Bahá'í children's class on the porch.

The three Bahá'í adults and seven children, ranging from four to sixteen, sat in a circle on the unpainted floor. For the boys and girls, all barefoot, being with the Bahá'ís was a 'dream-come-true'. They were wide-eyed, eager to do whatever those people, who seemed to have been dropped from the sky, wanted them to do.

They vied with one another to recite Bahá'í prayers by heart; and a few sang songs, encouraging the others and the adults to join in. When the children had sung every Bahá'í song they knew, they sang Negro spirituals. The northerners were particularly moved by 'Sweet Jesus, help me take one day at a time.'

During story-telling time, the northern man was inspired to create some tales on the spot. They were stories with Bahá'í themes, that required everyone to hold the hand of the person next to him. The children liked that, because they were affectionate. They didn't want to let go. A four-year-old boy was intrigued by the northern woman whose hand he was holding. He sat on her lap, looked at her hand, then glanced at his. He touched her hair and then kissed her cheek and cuddled up in her arms. The eleven-year-old girl placed her head on the woman's shoulder, looked into her eyes and whispered, 'Could you take me with you?'

The northern man was overwhelmed by the creativity of a six-year-old boy who shared several stories. *Bambi* was his favorite and he acted out every part, which included changing voices.

When the baby inside the house started screaming, the large woman came out and reprimanded the sixteen-year-old young woman for not providing milk for her infant. When the hostess offered to take the young woman to the grocery store, some of the children decided to play hopscotch with the northern woman; the others, including the six-year-old story-teller, opted to draw. But they didn't have any pencils or crayons or paper.

'Would you like me to draw you something?' the little story-teller asked the northern man.

'Sure', the man said.

The boy leaped from the porch and sped into the woods. Seconds later he raced back with a twig, brushed the sand away from the firm ground with his hand, and, using the twig as a drawing instrument, sketched the sun with its rays, then turned it into a smiling cat's face. He looked at what he had drawn, then looked at the man kneeling beside him and proceeded to create a story about a cat. With every picture the youngster drew, he made up a story.

'Remarkable', the northerner thought. 'If only I could record all of this.'

The hostess returned with the teenager, who had signed her declaration card while she had been away.

For the northern couple, it was difficult to leave, and sad in a way, because they wondered what was going to happen to those gifted, loving children. What chance did they have to develop their potential, to see and feel so much more than their parents had seen and felt? And there must be hundreds more like them – thousands.

As they slowly backed out of the driveway, with the children waving good-bye, the northern man noticed his hostess, behind the steering wheel, waving back. 'At least', he thought, 'they are going to see and be with that wonderful couple from time to time.' That lessened the heartache.

The Story of Jane Edmunds

Back at the Louis Gregory Institute the man from the north was able to attend to something very important, something he had looked forward to doing while planning the trip south. The day before he and his family were to return home he visited the Institute's cemetery. It was early morning. Though sunny, the normal heat peak of the day was at least five hours away. It was still, with the exception of the occasional song of a nearby bird.

There were only three grave sites; two had headstones, the other one didn't. And it was that one he was particularly interested in. Jane Edmunds's headstone wasn't ready, for she had been buried only a few weeks back. Her death had come unexpectedly.

He stood at the foot of her grave, closed his eyes and Jane came to mind; not in a still image, but, rather, in motion. After all, she had been a doer. He recalled her embracing people, teaching and serving, always giving her all.

She had been more than a successful black woman, a college-trained research chemist, an artist, living in a fine home in Eliot, Maine, and married to a physician; she was a universal woman who could fit comfortably in any situation or place; poor, rich, highly educated, unschooled – anyone – would feel comfortable with her. People were attracted to her because of her genuineness. In a world full of deceit, pretense, lies and chicanery, Jane was an example of a person succeeding and being happy without compromising the divine standards. Because of her steadfastness in the Faith, she became a leader, though not in any official sense. People simply respected and admired her, wanted to be with her and do as she did. It was something she wasn't aware of. In fact, in a letter to a Bahá'í friend shortly before her death, in which she described her experiences in South Carolina, Jane revealed her understanding of her spiritual condition: 'I hope from these experiences I will qualify for a prayer-scattering angel in the next world. This is a piddly Oklahoman.'

She went to South Carolina in early 1982, as she had gone in previous years, and as 'Abdu'l-Bahá would have gone – to help people. She could never get used to the poverty, not because it was personally distasteful, but because it prevented the poor rural blacks from realizing their potential, fulfilling their dreams, experiencing hope.

Because she felt that way, her approach to teaching was different from that of other travel teachers. She wanted to educate the poor blacks, lift their sights beyond their present condition, help them to understand that by being Bahá'ís they were participating in the mightiest undertaking in the world.

So she stressed the laws and obligations of the Faith, explaining as best she could the reasons for them. She shared with them the history of the Faith, describing Bahá'u'lláh's sufferings. Showing a film strip of people of different skin colors and cultures singing and clapping wasn't her idea of really educating the people. She felt it was more important to broaden their horizons than to arouse their emotions.

At first those who taught with her were aghast at her approach. But it worked. Some didn't dare try it, because they felt that only Jane Edmunds could reach the people that way. She shared the healing Message of Bahá'u'lláh as a physician prescribed medicine. She believed the Faith could help people, if not in this world, certainly in the next one.

Although she worked with the poor, Jane didn't dress like them. She wore what she would normally wear – designer clothes that she would make herself. Her clothes and accessories seemed an outward expression of her love for the arts, her world travels and depth of personality. She would have considered it condescending to enter a humble dwelling in different attire.

Most people would never have gone on a long trip if they had been in Jane's position. She had just recovered from pneumonia. Besides, she had a history of asthma. The hot humid climate of South Carolina could easily set off attacks. But she drove a Mercedes Benz with automatic shift and air-conditioning. That should help, she felt.

She had to go, because she had been there before. So many souls had been touched by Bahá'u'lláh and were yearning to learn more about the Faith. There were 224 Assemblies to be reformed and some new ones to establish, and so few to do the work in the field.

And it wasn't a matter of having little to do in the north. She was on Maine's District Teaching Committee, and taught the Faith in New England.

Jane Edmunds's trip was plagued by hardship from the start. Her Mercedes Benz broke down, throwing a rod. A major overhaul was required. Dealing with the white mechanics was an aggravating experience, because she had never grown accustomed to racism, whether she was the target – or someone else.

While the car was in the shop, she forged ahead in carrying out her assignment. In helping to elect Assemblies she had to search for the Bahá'ís on the back dirt roads, knocking on doors, often retracing her steps. One of her companions later said, 'Even when it seemed we had reached a dead end she never gave up. She seemed to be unaware of her handicap, or, should I say, determined to carry on in spite of it. I remember one time hoping she would quit as I was exhausted. Me, seventeen years younger and in good health! She was too busy telling the Concourse on High, "We've got to get this election done today – we can't come back tomorrow."'

One morning the nine or ten other travel teachers gained an insight into Jane's commitment to the project when she said to them: 'This is like the Conference of Bada<u>sh</u>t, and we must promise to meet here again next year.'

Jane seemed fearless; but she had her fears, which she managed to conceal from the native South Carolinians, because she didn't want to embarrass them. Her New England friend, who had joined her on the project, knew about her terrible fear of cockroaches.

Well, she encountered the insects, hordes of them, in a house where she was conducting an election. To compound the problem, she was stuck there for three hours, because the car she was using had broken down. Shortly after she called the Louis Gregory Institute to inform them of her car's breakdown – two hours from Hemingway – her friend from New England called back and asked if she was comfortable.

'Oh, yes, I'm comfortable', she said.

At eleven p.m. her friend and the project coordinator rescued Jane. On the way back, she related her experience to her friends: 'The cockroaches even came out during the daylight. Those cockroaches had no shame, no shame whatsoever.'

It was good to know that she and her colleagues were helping to build the administrative skeleton of the most populous Bahá'í district in the United States. But there were other rewards. Almost every time she ventured out, she returned to the Institute with a handful of signed declaration cards. To Jane, teaching someone the Faith was the ultimate in helping that person.

But the people she went to help often helped her. One event especially made an everlasting impression. It didn't occur on her last trip south. She had been in rural Georgia, calling on believers who hadn't been visited by other Bahá'ís for years. Their only link with the Bahá'í world was the *American Bahá'í*. Even if they couldn't read, the pictures inspired them. For many, the highlight of the month was going to the mailbox and finding the newspaper there.

It was an old black woman, a believer for ten years, who hadn't seen another Bahá'í for about that long, who proved to Jane that knowing how to read isn't necessary for an understanding of the core of the Faith or for firmness in the Covenant.

The woman shared with Jane her most precious possession, a piece of paper which she plucked from under her pillow. On it was the Noonday prayer, a gift from the travel teacher who had introduced her to Bahá'u'lláh.

Jane was moved by the way the woman held the paper, as if it were her only link with life. 'At noon time', the woman said, raising the paper above her head, 'I look at it and remember what that lady told me.' There was no doubt in Jane's mind that the prayer had been absorbed by that woman's pure heart.

South Carolina's assembly goals for 1982 had been achieved. 237 Assemblies had been formed, thanks to the valiant efforts of the small team of fieldworkers. In a sense, it was a miraculous accomplishment, considering the logistics involved and the fewness of their numbers.

Jane knew that they had been assisted. That awareness was expressed in an evaluation session that took place one evening in the Institute's women's dormitory shortly before the Riḍván period ended. There were only three women left, a Persian, the white New England friend and Jane. After a long day on the dusty road, they had showered and prepared for bed, but were too full of their work to sleep. They agreed that when out in the field they had sensed the power of the Concourse on High helping them accomplish what they had set out to do each day. And they had felt that power even when it had seemed impossible to find the people to hold the election. But in the end it had all worked, even if the election had had to be held under a tree, or the hood of a car used to count ballots.

They also agreed that confirmations come to us by giving up our puny wills for the will of God, and that unexpected benefits come from obedience to the laws of Bahá'u'lláh. There was no doubt in their minds Who was primarily responsible for the success of the consolidation campaign.

But Jane's ill-health took its toll. Just before she was due to go home to Maine she suffered a bad asthma attack. She managed to get to the door and push it open, then fell to her knees and cried out 'Yá Bahá'u'l-Abhá'. Two men heard her and came running out of their dormitory. One ran for help; the other one picked Jane up and carried her to a waiting car where she was placed in the administrator's arms. A young man, who had been Jane's partner for the last two weeks of the consolidation campaign, went along to the Air Force hospital, which was about an hour away from the Institute. But they never got there. When Jane fell into unconsciousness, they raced to a hospital thirty minutes closer. Jane never regained consciousness.

Who can evaluate such an event in its true perspective? To some it might seem a tragic waste of a life; yet, as one friend wrote, 'I must say that she died at the end of a project that was near and dear to her heart and at a time that she was very spiritually moved. She burned herself out for the love of Bahá'u'lláh. No greater joy could there ever be.'[41]

Now, recalling Jane's story, the northerner remembered her smile as she used to say, 'My heart is in South Carolina.' He glanced at the ground. Now it was truly there.

FOURTEEN

The Local Spiritual Assembly and Teaching

Though there are about 25,000 Local Spiritual Assemblies in the world, they are in varying degrees of maturity: some serve their communities effectively, others still struggle to meet regularly.

Obviously, the effectiveness of an LSA is based on its membership's commitment to regular deepening and prayer. An Assembly comprised of people all seriously involved in developing their spiritual natures is going to serve its community well and will understand why the Guardian felt that teaching was the Local Spiritual Assembly's primary responsibility.

Of course, for an Assembly that is plagued by consolidation problems, it will be difficult to implement the Guardian's suggestion on teaching even though it wants to. Marriage problems, the refereeing of personal disputes, the investigation of the source of local attacks on the Faith, as well as the organization of proclamation projects, seem to take up most of an Assembly's agenda. Realistically, that's a lot to ask of nine people who have jobs, families to bring up and homes to maintain. In consequence, finding the time and energy to develop a teaching plan and coordinate it turns into a monumental undertaking, one that usually isn't done; and if it is, it's done without much commitment, resulting in little or no success. And worse than that – the Assembly members are left plagued by guilt or teetering toward apathy.

Many Assemblies find it impossible to avoid such a condition, despite valiant efforts to change the direction in which they are heading. For the Assembly members it is a frustrating and painful situation, because deep down they feel they aren't doing what's right. Yet they can't pinpoint the problem.

However, for most Assemblies bogged down with the administration there's a simple answer. Unfortunately it isn't easily executed.

By directing most of an Assembly's time, energy and resources to teaching, it will eventually find itself heading in a healthier direction. An Assembly in New England that had been afflicted by personality feuds and mounting personal problems decided to direct most of its attention to teaching. With the help of an assistant to the Auxiliary Board, who encouraged the Assembly to focus on teaching, it experienced a spiritual rebirth. The load of personal problems lessened considerably, and personality feuds ended. When seekers started declaring their faith in Bahá'u'lláh, the Assembly members stopped berating themselves. They gained confidence and worked together with greater understanding and love. Experiencing victory after victory cleared the tension in the atmosphere of the Assembly chamber, and that helped to produce more efficient consultation and a happier community.

On the other hand, an Assembly with a strong record

in teaching decided to redirect its energy, virtually stopping all organized teaching. In a matter of months, the Assembly was besieged with personal problems. Discord broke out in the community, which led to people moving away, and the eventual dissolution of the Assembly.

Other Assemblies manage, year after year, to keep their administrative status by investing considerable energy in persuading Bahá'ís from other localities to move into their communities. Think what would happen if that energy were channeled into teaching. Those communities would certainly become more vital; and where there's spiritual vitality, there's usually spiritual growth on an individual basis and growth in the community as new believers are attracted to the Faith. In a way, an Assembly that maintains its numbers by encouraging out-of-towners to move in is like a hospital patient who is being kept alive by advanced medical technology. Of course, it is important to maintain our Assemblies, but ideally that is supposed to be done through teaching, not by artificial means. By continually relying on an annual campaign to recruit new Bahá'ís from other places, an Assembly risks turning the recruiting practice into a deeply entrenched habit, often replacing teaching as the primary source of community growth and stability.

It's understandable why an Assembly that concentrates mostly on solving community development problems harbors misconceptions about teaching, for it takes experience and considerable thinking about a subject to become proficient in it.

Often proclamation is mistaken for teaching. Organizing and carrying out a media campaign or holding a series of public meetings are considered teaching when, in fact, they are efforts to proclaim the Faith.

Usually in a community where there's an Assembly, it is the institution, not an individual, that produces a program for proclamation. Certainly all believers are encouraged to share with the Local Spiritual Assembly their ideas about proclamation; and this can be done at a Feast, in letters to the Local Assembly, or by meeting with the Assembly.

As for teaching – every believer has an obligation to teach, including each Assembly member. Generally, we don't have to gain approval from our Assembly to teach a neighbor, hold a fireside or go travel teaching. But an Assembly does have the responsibility to support those people who are already teaching and to encourage those who aren't. Support could come in the form of an encouraging note, or a telephone call from the teaching committee, offering assistance and sharing the Assembly's appreciation for whatever teaching effort a believer is making, regardless of how meager it seems. The Assembly could help in other ways: by assisting in finding speakers for firesides, or providing refreshments for some of the less-well-to-do friends who are holding firesides. The Assembly could pray regularly for the friends' teaching efforts, and pray also for those they are teaching. It could provide transportation to teaching events, and develop ways of nurturing the new believers.

Creating a Teaching Plan

One of the most important duties of an Assembly is to draft a community teaching plan and coordinate it.

Doing that takes more than good planning skills. Sensitivity is needed. And that's what a New York state Local Spiritual Assembly, serving a community of about a hundred men, women, and children, demonstrated.

Using the National Spiritual Assembly's teaching goals as a guide, and advice from an Auxiliary Board member and his assistant, the Assembly devised a way to create a realistic plan. First they decided to take stock of the resources within the local Bahá'í community. That was important, they felt, because without taking these into account, the Assembly might forge a plan that the community was incapable of implementing – something that had happened too often in the past. So the Assembly made an earnest attempt to determine the strengths of every believer in the community. That was done by asking the friends what they could contribute to the teaching program. Also, the Assembly relied on its own assessment of the friends' past performances, keeping in mind, of course, the possibility that people change.

The Assembly realized that in order to draw up a workable teaching plan it was essential to have a sound understanding of the ethnic, educational, economic and religious make-up of the town. With that kind of information, the Assembly felt, it could achieve a more intelligent, a more sensitive approach to teaching and proclamation. Without it, an Assembly would be like an archer trying to hit the 'bull's eye' with his eyes closed. Imagine, for instance, the kind of setback a Bahá'í community would suffer if its Assembly decided on a 'return of Christ' teaching theme in a town that was predominantly Jewish.

The Assembly found that learning its town's demographics didn't require an Assembly-sponsored house-to-house survey. The information was obtained from City Hall.

Since the Assembly adopted the attitude that it was a servant of the community, it felt obliged to share its findings with all the believers. It also believed it had to go to the community at large and seek its assistance in putting together a realistic teaching plan.

The Assembly decided to hold a special community-wide meeting, inviting all the Bahá'ís to attend. It was arranged far enough in advance to allow for ample promotion of the event.

There was an excellent turn-out. Not only were many good ideas offered to the Assembly, but enthusiasm among the friends was high – so high, that one veteran believer said she had never seen such unity and love among the friends. An Auxiliary Board member who had been monitoring the Assembly's efforts explained to the Assembly that by including the community in the development of the teaching plan, unity between the Assembly and the community was strengthened. Often, he said, when an Assembly disregards the community in creating a plan, it is perceived as an imperialistic agency, and resentment develops between the two, causing deep-seated hostility. By encouraging the community to make suggestions, the Assembly also ensures enthusiastic participation in implementing the teaching plan, because the friends are taking part in its creation – they have an investment in it.

After serious consideration of the community's suggestions and careful study of the demographics and resource data, the Assembly drew up a plan.

Since the city was relatively large, the Assembly decided not to try to teach in every section, but rather to concentrate in the three areas where the largest concentration of active Bahá'ís resided. To do otherwise, it was felt, would deplete their resources. Personal teaching and firesides were emphasized.

Realizing that not every believer felt confident enough to hold a fireside in his home, the Assembly decided to set up a community fireside, and encouraged everyone to participate in it. That was done in a variety of ways. Some elected to help clean the house where the meeting was held weekly, others prepared refreshments, while still others provided transportation to seekers or Bahá'ís who didn't have cars.

But the key element of the plan was for the friends to intensify their personal teaching efforts and use the fireside to expose seekers to a Bahá'í atmosphere. Usually that helps to draw them closer to Bahá'u'lláh.

It wasn't long before the friends started bringing seekers to the fireside: at times twenty or thirty came. Enrollments soon followed: about ten in a six-month period, and many other seekers were growing closer to the Faith. Fortunately, the plan called for the means to deepen the new believers. Those Bahá'ís closest to the newly-enrolled friends continued to shower love on them and serve them as they had in the past.

With that fireside firmly established, the Assembly started another one; and when it was well-rooted, still another was set in motion. By operating a phased fireside program, the Assembly felt more friends would gain confidence and courage to hold their own firesides on a more intimate basis.

One of the long-range goals of the Assembly was for its community to fulfill the Guardian's wish that everyone hold a fireside in his or her home at least once every nineteen days. But the Assembly was patient, realizing that the friends were at varying stages of development. For that reason, it prayed regularly for the success of the plan and the friends' spiritual growth.

The Assembly saw signs of growth, because a year after the plan was launched, friends at a Feast urged the Assembly to stress teaching more, and to provide them with more guidance on how to improve as teachers.

The Assembly responded quickly, because it realized that its plan wasn't perfect; and it was happy to see the enthusiasm for teaching among the friends, something it had hoped the plan would generate. Almost immediately, the Assembly decided to devote a special time for discussing teaching during the Feast, including stories of the believers' teaching experiences. It also organized a teaching conference, inviting an Auxiliary Board member to participate. And special teaching clinics were to be set up to help the friends perfect their one-to-one and fireside teaching skills.

Of course, the Assembly thanked the friends for their suggestions, and urged them to continue offering their ideas to the Assembly. By doing that, the Assembly strengthened the already strong bond between itself and the community.

A major factor in the Assembly's ability to devise a workable plan was its involvement with the assistant to the Auxiliary Board member for propagation. It wasn't a case of the assistant attending every Assembly meeting. There were periodic consultations, the first one occurring at the start of the planning stage. In fact, it was the assistant's suggestion to take stock of the community's resources and draw up a demographic profile of the city.

The Assembly felt at ease dealing with the assistant.

His visits were appreciated, because it was good to have an objective view of sticky issues. In some ways, it was like having a consultant to call on. He provided advice, and the Assembly was free to take it all, use part of it, or disregard it. What the Assembly did with his suggestions was of no consequence to the assistant. He was always available to help his assigned Assembly, gaining gratification from knowing that perhaps his help might strengthen an Assembly, and that the stronger an Assembly becomes, the stronger the Faith becomes.

Setting Realistic Goals

Although it is best if every Assembly has a teaching plan, not every one can be expected to be the same, because every community is different. Size is a factor. A community with only nine believers is obviously going to put together a less ambitious plan than a community with a hundred active believers. If it tries to operate like an Assembly with many Bahá'ís, the chances of fulfilling the goals of the plan are slim, and it could be psychologically damaging. Repeated defeat can lead to depression. By setting realistic goals and achieving them, confidence is generated among the believers. Without confidence, there's little chance of plans succeeding.

An Assembly in Texas almost experienced disaster from not meeting a goal. But fortunately what could easily have been devastating turned into a victory. For that to happen, a change in attitude and outlook was required.

For years the Assembly's teaching results had been meager: two or three enrollments a year through off-and-on-again firesides, potlucks, public meetings and sporadic personal teaching. The friends were frustrated, because they wanted their community to experience the kind of teaching victories that were occurring in Africa, Latin America and Asia. They longed to see the day when more than three people in their city would declare their belief in Bahá'u'lláh in a year. Some began to doubt whether that could ever happen.

During consultation one night, the Assembly decided to heed what Hand of the Cause of God Ṭarázu'lláh Samandarí had suggested at an area teaching conference: that when faced with what appear to be insurmountable obstacles the friends should recite the Remover of Difficulties 500 to 1,000 times a day, as Bahá'u'lláh had enjoined.[42]

'Let's try it!' the Assembly decided. In typical Texan style they tackled the biggest challenge. Every Assembly member vowed to say the prayer 1,000 times a day for nineteen days.

The challenge became a test. Ten days later, at the next Assembly meeting, they all admitted that they had been unable to keep their vow. It was a humbling experience. As one member pointed out, 'We weren't the super-saints we thought we were. We were unified, as never before, in our worthlessness.'

Though disappointed, they weren't crushed. In fact, during consultation, they realized how important it was to be aware of the Assembly's true capacity to do things at a given point in the institution's development. Perhaps future Assemblies in their city would be able to have each member recite the Remover of Difficulties 1,000 times a day throughout a Bahá'í month; but they realized that they couldn't; yet they wanted to follow the Hand of the Cause of God's appeal. After some deliberation, they wondered if Bahá'u'lláh would accept a less ambitious undertaking. With humility they decided to try it. Every member would say a hundred Remover of Difficulties a day and one member's spouse would say a hundred, making a grand total of 1,000 prayers daily for nineteen days. Because it was an honest offering, Bahá'u'lláh's guidance streamed into that city.

As a result, the first direct teaching was launched in Texas among the youth of that city. Seventy-five became Bahá'ís in three months. The Assembly was thrilled to know that Bahá'u'lláh had heard their prayers and had accepted them in their true state.

A Successful Teaching Plan

There's an Assembly in New England that has taken good advantage of its resources, creating a dynamic proclamation-teaching campaign that is not only attracting new believers but has generated a spirit of unity in the community that 'old-timers' have never experienced before.

There are no eloquent speakers in the community; no so-called 'teaching pundits'. But the community has exceptional musical talent – a married couple who are professionals. With encouragement from an Auxiliary Board assistant, the Assembly drew up a plan.

It decided to stage an outdoor concert in a section of the city that is undergoing changes. Essentially a poor neighborhood, composed of blacks, Puerto Ricans, whites and American Indians, some middle-class people were moving in to take advantage of the low-cost large old houses that were for sale. The Bahá'í musicians were among the group of inner-city pioneers.

The Assembly received permission to hold the concert in a vacant lot next to the city's Indian Council center. The master of ceremonies for the mid-afternoon Sunday affair was imported from a neighboring state. It was a Bahá'í, the Assembly felt, who would feel comfortable with the neighborhood and its people. Food and drink were served, but the kind of food and drink the local residents preferred – things like macaroni salad, and orange and grape soda. There was a cross-section of Bahá'í musicians playing their specialties: rhythm and blues, jazz, folk. Bahá'í and non-Bahá'í songs were sung. The performers were black and white, young and old.

The neighborhood rocked with tunes about love and unity. Windows opened and people leaned out to soak in the spirit of joy, some of them clapping to the musical rhythms. When neighborhood people were urged to come and join in the music-making, some came running out of their houses with tom-tom drums and other instruments – and performed. A bond was being built between the Bahá'ís and the people in that neighborhood. A couple of hundred men, women, and children pressed closer to the band stand, many sipping soda and eating macaroni salad, swaying happily to the music – black, white, Hispanic and Indian. A Bahá'í from another state, who had accompanied the master of ceremonies to the concert, had never experienced such a successful proclamation effort. It was successful, he felt, because it was not only an opportunity to share the name 'Bahá'í' with people, but it was an act of service. The people in the audience were more than entertained: they were exposed to and participated in an expression of racial and ethnic harmony they had never experienced before.

Some of the old-time Bahá'ís in the community were

amazed at what was unfolding before their eyes. Never in local Bahá'í history had such an effort of reaching out to others taken place.

Scores of people in the audience inquired about the Faith, taking pamphlets; almost everyone asked if the Bahá'ís would hold more concerts. The Assembly did arrange other concerts, some even in the winter. The Indian Council center was the site of one.

The Assembly decided to hold a community fireside at the Bahá'í musicians' home, which was in the heart of the neighborhood.

These firesides are organized with the customs of the neighborhood people in mind. While everyone gathers, people aren't sitting around, staring at their watches. They are mingling. Bahá'ís have an opportunity to make the seekers feel welcome and at ease.

Every fireside officially opens with a prayer which is usually sung by either the host or hostess. A different speaker is featured each week. Because of the fireside's reputation, the Assembly has no trouble getting speakers. And there's never a shortage of Bahá'ís, because they come in order to get a spiritual 'shot-in-the-arm'. Some travel seventy miles or more to be at the fireside. It is a topic of conversation at most Bahá'í functions in the state; and those community skeptics who felt the format wouldn't work have become the fireside's biggest boosters.

After the talk and the question and answer session, food is served and then more music is performed by the host and hostess or other musicians. There's no established ending time. No one who leaves is made to feel guilty. In fact, an easy come-and-go atmosphere prevails. It's set up that way because that's the way the local residents operate. There have been times when firesides have lasted until two or three in the morning.

Since the host and hostess are professional musicians, they are on the road a great deal and can't always be home on the fireside night. That doesn't deter them from holding the teaching event. Assembly representatives act as host and hostess. Continuity, the Assembly feels, is important, because to some of the seekers it is the high point of their week, providing the kind of spiritual food they can't find elsewhere.

The concerts continue. Certainly not as often as the firesides. To the Assembly, the concerts help to prepare the soil, while the firesides plant and cultivate the seeds.

After a few months of firesides, six people enrolled. Word has spread throughout the neighborhood that at the house where the Bahá'ís gather, everyone is really welcomed and loved.

FIFTEEN

How to Teach

Remember the young man in buffalo skin pants, who found and lost the teaching touch? After a ten-year search, including a pioneering stint in the Arctic, he found it again in — of all places — the town in which he was reared and from which he had run away several times. Rediscovery came during a private conversation with a close Bahá'í friend.

Today he's aware of how people become and remain enkindled. He works at it every day, because he understands now that that's what is needed in order to keep the fire of the love of God burning within him. He's convinced that without daily prayer and deepening the fire would die. Since his rediscovery, teaching opportunities come his way, sometimes in the strangest places and under the strangest circumstances.

One day a friend, an automobile mechanic who was working on the Bahá'í's car, noticed an open copy of the *Kitáb-i-Íqán* on the front seat. When he picked it up, he had difficulty returning to his work. The Revelation captivated him. 'Please get me a copy', the mechanic said to the Bahá'í.

There have been other exciting teaching incidents in his life, and he's no longer surprised when they occur. Now he realizes that teaching is really a simple process, and he feels more capable of carrying out Bahá'u'lláh's advice on teaching:

A kindly approach and loving behavior toward the people are the first requirements for teaching the Cause. The teacher must carefully listen to whatever a person has to say – even though his talk may consist only of vain imaginings and blind repetitions of the opinions of others. One should not resist or engage in argument. The teacher must avoid disputes which will end in stubborn refusal or hostility, because the other person will feel overpowered and defeated. Therefore, he will be more inclined to reject the Cause. One should rather say, 'Maybe you are right, but kindly consider the question from this other point of view.' Consideration, respect, and love encourage people to listen and do not force them to respond with hostility. They are convinced because they see that your purpose is not to defeat them, but to convey truth, to manifest courtesy, and to show forth heavenly attributes. This will encourage the people to be fair. Their spiritual natures will respond, and, by the bounty of God, they will find themselves recreated.

Consider the way in which the Master teaches the people. He listens very carefully to the most hollow and senseless talk. He listens so intently that the speaker says to himself, 'He is trying to learn from me.' Then the Master gradually and very carefully, by means that the other person does not perceive, puts him on the right path and endows him with a fresh power of understanding.[43]

The Master's whole life was a teaching effort. Nursing the sick, feeding the poor, communicating with his children, or strolling alone on the slopes of Mt. Carmel were acts of teaching. 'Abdu'l-Bahá worked at living the life, and attracted the true seeker to Himself wherever He went. And he wanted us to do the same, nothing more.

Teaching and the Bahá'í Home

Creating and maintaining a Bahá'í home, regardless of where we live, is doing what the Master did. By a Bahá'í home is meant a place where all the family are working faithfully at loving and knowing God, are sincerely trying to make His standards part of their being, are developing divine virtues, are earnestly striving to share His Message with others. It is a place where all who enter feel accepted, respected and loved. It is a rescue station for the sick-at-heart and spiritually starving. It is a lighthouse for the seekers of truth. In a Bahá'í home, every child who enters, regardless of his origin and background, is treated as a family member. Such a home is a growing center of spirituality where discussion of the Teachings between parents and children is commonplace, where prayer is a natural practice and the Creative Word is viewed as the source of illumination and inspiration.

There are homes like this in different parts of the world, in various forms – huts, tents, hogans, high-rise apartments and one-family dwellings in middle-class neighborhoods – all blessed by a similar spirit.

The Example of Allan Raynor

Canadian Allan Raynor lived in such a home. From the outside it appeared like most other houses in suburban Toronto. But the difference became apparent upon entering. Almost immediately you felt welcome, that you belonged there. Africans, orientals, Indians, poor, rich, unschooled and highly-educated shared the same feeling. It was as if the Raynor home really belonged to everyone. Those who knew Allan well would probably agree that that's the way he would want his home remembered. But they would remember other things: for years, the weekly firesides, the deepenings, the family's spiritual battles fought and mostly won. But what really stood out was the firmness of belief that permeated the home.

Allan was relatively tall and slim, and wore a hearing aid. Though a heavy smoker, and a hard-driving insurance salesman – one of Canada's best – he seemed to be aware of a tremendous secret that made him smile all the time.

Allan had never been to college, and would be the first to admit that he wasn't a scholar. Yet the friends throughout Canada sought his services as a teacher of the Faith. One of his favorite subjects was the Covenant. Undoubtedly, his success in teaching that topic came from his own example of firmness. Another reason why he grew to be so popular among the believers was his easy accessibility, even when he was a member of Canada's National Spiritual Assembly. He always found time to share with others whatever knowledge he had about the Writings. His greatest pleasure came from serving; and those he served were moved by his quiet kindness and generosity.

Of those who benefited from his help, some shared their gratitude in letters to him:

When Stephen suffered a frightening convulsion, you quickly found the best specialist to treat him. When Jack, as an enthusiastic but untried Bahá'í, was determined to further his education in the then trouble-ridden city of Paris, dangerous in some respects to even very strong Bahá'ís, you were concerned enough, as a measure of protection, to make a special point of counseling him before his departure. When Mary Lou and her husband were in hospital, you traveled a long way to visit and cheer them. (They have not forgotten this.) And when I, myself, was hospitalized, almost too ill to know you were beside my bed, the hazy knowledge of your presence lifted my heart and I was comforted and grateful for your support . . .[44]

Allan's inclination to help others extended to the business world. Many salesmen sought his advice, and they respected the Bahá'í Faith because they respected him. They knew how much the Faith meant to him, because he was open about his beliefs. He was, as a Toronto businessman said, '. . . above all a very honest person in his dealings with others. If Al said he was going to do something, it was done . . . There was no deceit about the man. You always knew where the man stood, and you took what he said at face value.'[45]

Whatever wisdom Allan had attained was the result of his study of the Writings. In that regard he was very much like his close friends Curtis Kelsey and George Spendlove. Most of his Bahá'í books contained many underlined passages and personal annotations along the margins, undoubtedly insights that came from meditating on what he had read. Of all his books, the *Gleanings from the Writings of Bahá'u'lláh* was his favorite, taken with him wherever he went.

In 1977 he had a cancerous bladder removed, and the prognosis wasn't good. Hand of the Cause of God John Robarts's frequent visits to the hospital bolstered Allan's spirit, for it was the Hand of the Cause who had taught him the Faith. Almost every Sunday until the end, Allan would receive a phone call from John Robarts, even when the latter was in Africa.

Although Allan had retired from work two years earlier, he was as busy as ever, channeling most of his energy into Bahá'í projects. Deep down he knew that conquering cancer, especially at his age, would be difficult, maybe impossible. But he was going to give it his all. Giving up smoking wasn't easy. It rarely is for a chain smoker. But Allan did it. He wanted to live, for there was unfinished business: a son, a sensitive young man, needed more guidance. How Allan wanted to help him! But that required time. There was the Five Year Plan and its many goals that had to be won. There was his own spiritual development. His greatest fear was not remaining steadfast in his faith and keeping his commitment with God. To others, however, he was a pillar of faith, someone they could lean on, especially when weary with fighting their spiritual battles. Those who spent time with him, even when he was ill, usually left spiritually fortified. Perhaps it was that fear of failing to be steadfast that drove him to grow more and more dependent on the Creative Word, and that gave him an inner strength he wasn't conscious of. Allan wanted so to please God.

On 21 March, 1979, the doctor told him that he had six months to live: the cancer had spread to his brain. When the pain intensified, he held back from taking pain-killing drugs. Instead he contacted the Universal House of Justice to seek its guidance on whether it was permissible to take narcotic-based medicine.

Impressed with Allan's attitude, Canada's Cancer Society asked him to participate in a film about coping with the dreaded disease. So much of what he had to say was so significant that he turned out to be the film's major participant. When told jokingly by a Society representative that he had become a movie star, Allan blushed and said, 'No, I don't want to become a star.'

He had consented to be in the film so that other cancer victims would be exposed to the Faith's views on healing and death. He was convinced that there was no better way to serve those who were terminally ill. Truly, his participation in the making of the film was an act of service. The project producers knew that – and they also knew it was why Allan's contribution was so effective.

His battle against cancer wasn't easy for his wife and four children, even though they shared his views of death. They had always been a close family, all linked by a deep love for each other. To know that in a few months Allan wouldn't be home again was a thought that hurt. Oh, they had had their spats, but he was the magnet of the family. When in trouble, they would invariably come to him for help. And in a way he helped them, and everyone else who was close to him, to endure his last six months with dignity and spiritual understanding. His eldest son's Father's Day letter seemed to reflect the family's feelings about Allan and his struggle.

Dear Dad,

Rather than sending you some token of love and affection on Father's Day it seemed that a more spiritual gift – this letter – would bind us more closely together, and for just a brief moment, perhaps, dispel a bit of that lonely feeling.

Our visit together in May confirmed a kind of spiritual union between us that has been developing since the earliest beginnings of my being. It is an indissoluble union. It has been tempered by tests and it has grown through your deep, abiding and patient love for me. It continues to grow as I mature and am more able to reciprocate in kind the love you offer to me, to my family, to our family and to our friends.

You will always be with us even as you and I are together now in spirit. By mere efforts of will and reflection we hurl aside barriers of time and space. Already the physical need of tangible presence seems to be falling aside, and will continue to wither, as our spiritual union deepens and broadens to include those about us on this plane, and those eager souls yearning to encourage, support and help us, those souls already members of the Concourse on High in the Abhá Kingdom. In the realm of light and vision, when the irksome veil of the physical world has fallen aside like some abandoned chrysalis, the bonds of love already established will strengthen.

Then there will be no thought of loneliness. Even now, you are not alone. Your families of children and friends will always be only a thought away. And when, and if, you call me, I'll be there . . .[46]

The way in which Allan prepared for his journey to the 'next world' moved many hospital staff members and impressed one of Canada's leading newspapers so much that it published a long feature story about him. The nurses remember how Allan comforted other cancer patients. He seemed to sense their inability to share their fear of dying. And when he brought up the subject and explained, in a sympathetic way, what death really was, many of the patients felt as if a great weight had been lifted from their hearts. Allan's reputation spread.

Perhaps the high point of his six-month vigil was a visit from an old friend who was living in the Holy Land. This member of the Universal House of Justice, who had been sent on a special mission to North America, was also directed by the Supreme Institution to deliver a message personally to Allan. Before saying good-bye, the friend said, 'Allan, the House wants you to be an example – to flame out.'

The next day Allan Raynor didn't seem like a man who

had about three months to live. He made travel plans and was enthusiastic about teaching and holding study classes on the Covenant. The fact that the summer school in Sylvan Lake, Alberta, was about 2,000 miles from home didn't deter him. He taught a course there, and met with his son in nearby Red Deer – the son he wanted so much to help. At Canada's National Center in Ontario he gave a seminar on the Covenant. In Nova Scotia he held a two-day study class. As the friends filed out of that meeting, Allan's eldest son heard his father say, 'Well, that's it. It's done. It's finished.'

But Allan Raynor's teaching work wasn't done, even though the day after he returned home he had to be rushed to the hospital. The nurses sensed that someone special was in their midst, not only because of the large number of visitors streaming into Allan's room. There was something about his face that impressed them, too. He seemed so happy. It was a special kind of happiness that most people don't feel, but are seeking.

One visitor, a close friend, who had been married to a Bahá'í for many years, but who hadn't joined the Faith, signed her declaration card a few days after visiting Allan. An old man, who had come to visit Allan for about two minutes, stayed for six hours, leaving with a new understanding of the meaning of life.

Seventeen people, not all of them Bahá'ís, visited Allan Raynor on his last day. He talked about the Faith, even with his doctor, who had grown to admire Allan. As the physician leaned toward his dying friend, Allan said, 'Bill, you're missing the greatest thing in the world, and don't forget I told you.'

After Allan's wife left the room around midnight, her daughter, a nurse, took over watching her father. She sensed he was fading fast. The thought that she had recently been the cause of joy to him cheered her heart. It wasn't anything she had given him, or had said to him. When she was a baby, he had made a wish that he would live to witness her twenty-first birthday. And that had occurred two weeks earlier.

Around two-thirty in the morning, she watched her father reach out for the *Gleanings*, touch it, smile and pass away.

References

1 Bahá'u'lláh, *Gleanings from the Writings of Bahá'u'lláh*, trans. Shoghi Effendi, Wilmette, Bahá'í Publishing Trust, 2nd rev. edn, 1976, no. CXXXIV

2 Shoghi Effendi, *Citadel of Faith*, Wilmette, Bahá'í Publishing Trust, 1965, p. 140

3 'Abdu'l-Bahá, *Tablets of the Divine Plan*, Wilmette, Bahá'í Publishing Trust, rev. edn, 1977, p. 7

4 'Abdu'l-Bahá, cited by the Universal House of Justice in a letter to all National Spiritual Assemblies dated March 3, 1977, *The Individual and Teaching – Raising the Divine Call*, Wilmette, Bahá'í Publishing Trust, 1977, p. vii

5 Abu'l-Faḍl Gulpáygání, *Miracles and Metaphors*, trans. Juan Ricardo Cole, intro. Amin Banani, Los Angeles, Kalimát Press, 1981, pp. x–xi

6 Letter on behalf of Shoghi Effendi, cited in *The Individual and Teaching*, p. 30, no. 80

7 'Abdu'l-Bahá, cited in *The Divine Art of Living*, New York City, Brentano Publishers, 1926, p. 78

8 'Abdu'l-Bahá, *Tablets of 'Abdu'l-Bahá*, vol. 2, p. 348. Chicago, Bahá'í Publishing Society, 2nd edn, 1919.

9 'Abdu'l-Bahá, *The Will and Testament of 'Abdu'l-Bahá*, Wilmette, Bahá'í Publishing Committee, 1944, p. 25

10 Bahá'u'lláh, *The Kitáb-i-Íqán*, Wilmette, Bahá'í Publishing Trust, 2nd edn, 1950, p. 31

11 Matt. 7:16

12 *Gleanings*, no. CXXXVI

13 Bahá'u'lláh in *Bahá'í Prayers*, Wilmette, Bahá'í Publishing Trust, 1982, p. 129

14 'Abdu'l-Bahá, cited in *The Divine Art of Living*, comp. Mabel Hyde Paine, Wilmette, Bahá'í Publishing Trust, 1960, p. 26

15 'Abdu'l-Bahá, cited in *Spiritual Foundations: Prayer, Meditation, and the Devotional Attitude*, Wilmette, Bahá'í Publishing Trust, 1980, p. 8, no. 22

16 *Gleanings*, no. LXXXII
17 *Kitáb-i-Íqán*, p. 3
18 Bahá'u'lláh, 'Tablet of Aḥmad', *Bahá'í Prayers*, p. 212
19 Pilgrim's note cited in *Principles of Bahá'í Administration*, London, Bahá'í Publishing Trust, 3rd edn, pp. 90–91, 1973
20 Bahá'u'lláh, *The Hidden Words*, Wilmette, Bahá'í Publishing Trust, Rp 1982, p. 33, no. 33, Persian
21 Bahá'u'lláh, cited in *Spiritual Foundations*, p. 1, no. 1
22 *Gleanings*, no. LXXIX
23 'Abdu'l-Bahá, cited in *Divine Art of Living*, 1960, p. 39
24 Bahá'u'lláh, *Spiritual Foundations*, p. 1, no. 2
25 Ibid.
26 *Gleanings* no. CXXXVI
27 'Abdu'l-Bahá, cited in *Divine Art of Living*, 1960, p. 78
28 *Gleanings*, no. CXXV
29 Letter on behalf of Shoghi Effendi, cited in *Individual and Teaching*, p. 40, no. 116. Underlining mine, for emphasis.
30 'Abdu'l-Bahá, cited in May Maxwell, *An Early Pilgrimage*, Oxford, George Ronald, 1953, p. 42
31 From a letter by Martha Root written from Czechoslovakia on 26 November 1935
32 Cited in *Pioneer Post*, Wilmette, International Goals Committee of the National Spiritual Assembly of the United States, June 1982, vol. 5, no. 1
33 'Abdu'l-Bahá, cited in *Individual and Teaching*, p. 13, no. 30
34 'Abdu'l-Bahá, cited in Rúḥíyyih Rabbani, *A Manual for Pioneers*, New Delhi, Bahá'í Publishing Trust, 1974, p. 4
35 Shoghi Effendi, cited in *Principles of Bahá'í Administration*, p. 11
36 'Be a home for the stranger, a balm to the suffering . . .', *Gleanings*, no. CXXX
37 From a letter to the author
38 Nathan Rutstein, *He Loved and Served*, Oxford, George Ronald, 1982, pp. 128–9
39 'Abdu'l-Bahá, *Selections from the Writings of 'Abdu'l-Bahá*, comp. Research Department of the Universal House of Justice, Haifa, Bahá'í World Centre, 1978, p. 270, no. 217
40 'Abdu'l-Bahá, *The Promulgation of Universal Peace*, Wilmette, Bahá'í Publishing Trust, 1982, p. 214

41 From a letter to the author dated 30 June 1982
42 See Shoghi Effendi, *God Passes By*, Wilmette, Bahá'í Publishing Trust, rev. edn, 1974, p. 119
43 Quoted by Ḥájí Mírzá Ḥaydar-'Alí, *Stories from the Delight of Hearts*, trans. A. Q. Faizi, Los Angeles, Kalimát Press, 1980, pp. 109–10. These are not the exact words of Bahá'u'lláh, but convey the sense of what He said.
44 From a letter to Allan Raynor dated 17 May 1979
45 *Toronto Globe Mail*, 26 Sept. 1979
46 From a letter to Allan Raynor dated 14 June 1979